GCSE RE For You

Christianity and Moral Issues

Anne Jordan

Stanley Thornes (Publishers) Ltd

Text © Anne Jordan 1999

Printed in Hong Kong by Wing King Tong
Page make-up by Pentacor PLC, High Wycombe
Illustrated by Jane Taylor, Richard Duszczak and Steve Ballinger
Picture research by Helen Reilly

Original line illustrations © Stanley Thornes (Publishers) Ltd 1999
The right of Anne Jordan to be identified as author of this work has
been asserted by her in accordance with the Copyright, Designs and Patents Act 1988.

First published in 1999 by:
Stanley Thornes (Publishers) Ltd
Ellenborough House
Wellington Street
CHELTENHAM GL50 1YW
England

99 00 01 02 03 / 10 9 8 7 6 5 4 3 2 1

A catalogue record for this book is available from the British Library.

ISBN 0-7487-4039-2

Acknowledgements
With thanks to the following for permission to reproduce photographs and other
copyright material in this book:
AKG: 35; Barnardo's Photographic Archive: 77; Circa: 118; Commission for Racial
Equality (UK): 84; The *Daily Mail*/Solo Syndication: 29; Greenpeace: 51; Help the
Aged: 79; Hulton Getty: 23, 34, 96; Mary Evans Picture Library: 21; Oxfam: *John
Taylor* 102; Panos Pictures: *Nancy Durrell-McKenna* 111, 112; Rex Features Ltd: 8, 12
(left and middle), 24 (top), 38, 57, 59, 74, 78, 83, 90, 91, 115, 117, 122; Science
Photo Library: *John Greim* 4, *Petit Format* 59, *Will Mc Intyre* 95, *Sheila Terry* 125
(top), *Damien Lovegrove* 125 (bottom); Still Pictures: *A Arbib* 103, *Steve Lewis* 104,
Mark Edwards 105; Tear Fund: 53; Tony Stone Worldwide: 73.

Contents

Definitions of Morality

What do you think?

Look at the following situations and decide which person has acted in the right way and which person's behaviour was wrong.

Situation A

Jenny and Emma, two sisters, have agreed to visit their grandfather in hospital. The older sister, Jenny, is invited to the cinema at the last moment. She asks her sister to lie to their grandfather by telling him she could not come as she has a cold. But Emma tells her grandfather the truth that Jenny has gone to the cinema.

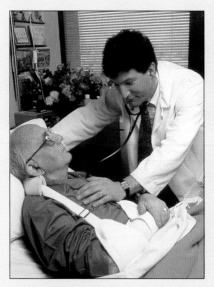

Which sister's action was right?

Situation B

David and Ian want to become members of a gang. The gang informs them that the initiation ceremony involves stealing cigarettes from the local shop. David refuses as he does not believe stealing is ever right. Ian goes ahead with the initiation but the shopkeeper catches him when he tries to steal the cigarettes. He receives a caution from the police.

Activity

Discuss your decision for each situation with your teacher and the rest of the class.

Was it worth it?

When you made your decision, you thought about each person's conduct and the rules for right and wrong behaviour. You decided what form of behaviour is right and what form is wrong. You made a **moral** decision.

Some Christians believe that God has given people a free choice of how to behave. God has given them the **free will** to behave according to their moral conscience.

Other Christians believe that a moral decision is caused (**determined**) by their genetic inheritance and the environment in which they were brought up. These Christians do not believe that people have free will.

Christians base their moral code on what they believe to be God's laws. The moral code for Christians is formed by the way in which they interpret the laws and teaching found in the Bible. Some Christians interpret this code for themselves. Other Christians follow the code as taught to them by their church leaders.

Christians have based much of their moral code on the **Ten Commandments**. The Ten Commandments could be summarized as:

1   You must have only one God.

2   You must have no idols or images.

3   You must not treat God's name with disrespect.

4   You must keep the Sabbath as a holy day.

5   You must treat your parents with respect.

6   You must not kill.

7   You must not commit adultery.

8   You must not steal.

9   You must not lie about other people.

10   You must not want what other people have.

What is ...?

Morality is conduct based on the distinction between right and wrong.

Determinism is the belief that we do not have free will. The cause of an event is outside our control.

Ethics is the study of how people behave as regards right and wrong conduct. Ethics is the study of morality.

Activity

I   Discuss with your teacher and the rest of the class which commandments seem relevant for today, and which commandments many people no longer obey.

2   Discuss the reasons why you think some commandments are ignored in today's society.

Questions

I   Explain the term 'morality'.

2   What are 'ethical' questions?

3   If you could add an eleventh commandment to the list, what would it be and why? Explain the reasons for your choice of commandment in some detail.

Topic 2

Ethics in practice

Agape is Christian love. Jesus taught that love of God includes loving your neighbour as yourself. Christians must act out of unconditional love in every action they take. If someone who needs help is ignored, then they believe God is ignored.

Philosophers have tried to solve the problem of knowing how to behave in a moral way. They have developed different ethical theories to help people make moral decisions, and to provide them with a framework for dealing with moral questions.

Some philosophers look at the **motives** of an action to decide whether it is moral – for example, does it show love of others? For other philosophers it is the **consequences** of people's actions which need to be considered.

Situation ethics

Situation ethics is a theory developed by Joseph Fletcher in the 1960s. It attempts to develop a guide to how to behave in the right way, which could be applied to each situation or circumstance. Joseph Fletcher said that an action is morally right if the intention is to show Christian love. The consequences of an action might not turn out as intended, but if the motive behind the action was love then it is a morally right act. Fletcher suggests that certain acts, such as lying and murder, may be morally right, depending on the situation.

Jesus taught people to love their neighbour

 What do you think?

A couple has fostered a four-year-old child for three years. The child has a happy and secure home. The foster parents put in an application to adopt the child, which is turned down. The local authority is not prepared to consider them as adoptive parents because they are over forty, and the authority has a rule that people over forty are too old to be parents.

What do you think would be the most loving outcome for the child? Would your decision be the same if it was based on the principles of situation ethics? Would the local authority have arrived at a different decision if it had used situation ethics?

The Golden Rule

> *Do to others as you would have them do to you.* (Luke 6:31)

Activity

1 Common to all religions is the Golden Rule.
   a Read Luke 6:31 and in your own words state the rule.
   b Explain why you think it has been called the 'Golden Rule'.
2 a Find out about the work of an agency which seeks to help people in trouble.
   b Design a poster, advert or the opening page of their website to help the organization to persuade people to support their work.

Utilitarianism

The theory of utilitarianism was developed by Jeremy Bentham (1748–1832) and John Stuart Mill (1806–73). According to their theory, the consequences of an action should be considered, rather than its motives. If the consequences of an action result in the greatest happiness for the greatest number of people, then the action is morally right. Rule utilitarianism and Act utilitarianism are two forms of this philosophy.

Rule utilitarianism judges the morality of an action according to the consequence of everybody breaking the rule. Rule utilitarians believe there is far greater happiness for the majority in a society if everyone keeps a particular rule. It would be morally wrong to break a rule if that rule is for the benefit of society as a whole. Therefore everyone, regardless of the situation, must keep all rules.

Act utilitarianism judges the morality of an action according to the consequences of that action. The action that results in the greatest happiness for the greatest number is the action that an act utilitarian would judge to be morally right in that specific situation. The rule is applied to each individual situation, and there may be times when better consequences are achieved by ignoring the rule.

What is ...?

Rule utilitarians believe that by always keeping to the rule, whatever the situation, then the course of action will be morally right. Such a belief is called **absolute morality**.

Act utilitarians look at each individual situation to decide what is the best course of action to make the action morally right. This may mean breaking the rules on some occasions. This is called **relative morality**.

What do you think?

Should you always keep your promises? Rule utilitarians would answer, 'Yes, because this results in the greatest happiness for the greatest number of people.' Act utilitarians would look at each situation to make the decision whether or not to keep a promise.

Are there ever situations when it would be morally right to break a promise?

Activity

In small groups, work out two situations, which involve telling a lie, to present to the rest of the class.

Include one situation where the consequence of telling a lie seems to be morally right and one situation where the consequence of telling a lie seems to be morally wrong.

Christians try to live their lives according to the teaching of Jesus, but they may do this in different ways. Some Christians believe their role is to pray for those in need and to raise money to give practical aid. Other Christians believe that they must take a more active role in improving the lives of people who are less fortunate than themselves in some way.

 Activity

> On one occasion, Jesus said that God had chosen him 'to bring good news to the poor … to proclaim liberty to the captives and recover sight for the blind; to set free the oppressed'.
>
> Explain in your own words the four things Jesus said that he had to do in the world.

Liberation theology

Liberation theology is a moral philosophy that teaches that Christians must help to free people from injustice. It teaches that Christians must not only help to save people's souls but also help them to achieve freedom from oppression and exploitation. According to liberation theology, a belief in God requires people to improve the quality of life for the less fortunate.

Liberation theology is popular in Latin American countries. Here, 90 per cent of the people live in poverty and struggle every day to have enough money on which to live. The aim of liberationists is to change the lives of the poor so that they can achieve a better quality of life. And this means that these societies will have to change: if the poor are to have a better standard of living then the rich will have to give up some of their wealth.

Sometimes their attempts to change things in Latin America have brought Christians into conflict with the government of these countries. Oscar Romero, for example, the Roman Catholic archbishop in El Salvador, was assassinated in March 1980 because of his support for the oppressed people of his country.

 Activity

> 1 Find out as much as you can about Oscar Romero.
> 2 Write a newspaper report of his death, explaining how his religious beliefs influenced his work. Think about including the views of his associates or friends, any witnesses to his death and an official government spokesperson.

Oscar Romero

'*May Christ's sacrifice give us the courage to offer our bodies for justice and peace.*'

(The last words of Oscar Romero)

1 Explain, in your own words, what you think Oscar Romero meant by his final words.
2 Romero said that if he were killed, he would 'rise again in the people of El Salvador'. Since 1991, El Salvador has had a democratic government. Do you think that Oscar Romero's sacrifice was worthwhile?

Duty is the binding force of what is right. If people follow their duty, they behave in a way that they think is right according to morality or conscience. It is the morally right thing to do in a situation.

People use words such as 'ought' and 'must' when discussing moral issues. There are different views as to where people's ideas of morality come from. One view is that people's ideas of right and wrong are born in them. These people just know what is good and what is bad behaviour. Others regard **conscience** as the voice of God telling people how to behave in a morally right way.

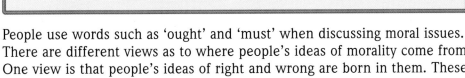

In a small group, or with your teacher, discuss the following questions.

• Why do we have to behave in a moral way?
• Why can't we do just what we want?
• Why should we not steal if we feel like it?
• Why should we not stay out all night even if our parents have told us to be in at 11 pm?

1 Explain what decides whether an action is morally right or wrong for:
   a Situation ethics
   b A rule and an act utilitarian
   c A liberation theologian.
2 a What does the word 'agape' mean?
   b How do you think a Christian might be able to show agape in their everyday life?
3 What do you think the following people would understand by the phrase 'doing their duty'?
   a a soldier
   b a nurse
   c a parent
4 Does following our conscience mean simply doing what we want? Give reasons for your answer.
5 Besides the Ten Commandments, what other factors should influence the way in which a Christian comes to a moral decision? Support your answer with reasons and examples.

Do you understand...

how Christians make moral decisions?

Task 1

Look at the list of decisions below. Write down which of these are moral decisions. Explain why you have decided that they are moral decisions.

a Which clothes to wear to a party.
b Whether or not to ask your best friend to come to the party.
c Whether to tell the truth about the fact you do not like your friend's new hairstyle.
d Whether to flirt with your best friend's boyfriend/girlfriend.
e Whether or not to arrive home at the time set by your parents.
f What to have for breakfast on the day following the party.
g Whether or not to return the money your friend lent you for the taxi fare home.

Task 2

The following people have to make ethical decisions in the course of their work. For each person, explain the ethical decisions they may have to make.

a a doctor
b a politician
c a genetic biologist
d a priest/minister

Task 3

A rule utilitarian believes that it is possible to make a rule to cover all similar situations. Keeping to the rule is the morally right action.

1 List and explain any rules you can think of which would be regarded as absolute by a rule utilitarian.
2 How does the moral decision-making of an act utilitarian differ from that of a rule utilitarian?
3 Do you think that utilitarianism is the best way to make an ethical decision? Consider in your answer the strengths and weaknesses of the theory.

Task 4

1 Look back at the section explaining situation ethics. How are situation ethics and act utilitarianism similar in the way in which moral decisions are made?
2 Why do some people believe that situation ethics is the most appropriate way for Christians to make moral decisions?

> If I speak in the tongues of men and of angels, but have not love, I am only a resounding gong or a clanging cymbal. If I have the gift of prophecy and can fathom all mysteries and all knowledge, and if I have a faith that can move mountains, but have not love, I am nothing. If I give all I possess to the poor and surrender my body to the flames, but have not love, I gain nothing. Love is patient, love is kind. It does not envy, it does not boast, it is not proud. It is not rude, it is not self-seeking, it is not easily angered, it keeps no record of wrongs. Love does not delight in evil but rejoices with the truth. It always protects, always trusts, always hopes, always perseveres. Love never fails.
>
> (1 Corinthians 13:1–8)

Task 5

1 What type of love is St Paul describing?
2 What qualities does St Paul believe that this type of love possesses?
3 How might St Paul's description of love be linked to the moral code of situation ethics?
4 In earlier translations of this passage the word 'charity' was used instead of love.

   a Why do you think modern writers chose to use the word 'love' instead of 'charity'?
   b Would the word 'charity' make the passage more or less relevant to people supporting liberation theology? Give reasons for your view.

Task 6

1 Why do some people believe that religion and morality are related to each other?
2 Why do you think that some people believe that if everybody kept the last five of the Ten Commandments we would live in a more moral society?
3 'Christians should not be involved in politics.' Do you agree? Give reasons for your answer, showing that you have thought about more than one point of view.

Topic 1

Aims and types of punishment

Rules, laws and punishments

1 Study the photographs on this page. What crime is being committed in each case?
2 Make a list of the possible reasons why people commit crimes.

 What do you think?

1 What rules does your school have?
2 Why do we have school rules?
3 Should we punish people who break school rules?
4 Are there any school rules that you think are pointless?
5 Are there any rules that you think your school should add to its list?

You come across rules in school every day. Society also has rules, which are needed for people to live and work together successfully. Rules for the local community, made by a local authority, are called **by-laws**. Rules for the whole country, made by Parliament, are called **laws**.

When someone breaks the law the punishment is more than lines or an hour's detention after school. The type of punishment that offenders are given depends on the seriousness of the crime that has been committed. It also depends on the aim of the punishment.

The aims of punishment

Punishments for breaking the laws are decided and laid down by the legal and justice system. Criminal courts hear cases, and punishments are decided after the accused person has been found guilty of breaking the law. There are four main theories of punishment, each of which has a different aim.

Theory of punishment	Aim of punishment	Examples of punishment
1 Protection	To protect society from somebody's anti-social behaviour by stopping him or her from repeating their actions.	A driving ban for dangerous driving; a long prison sentence for dangerous offenders.
2 Retribution (revenge)	To give a punishment that fits the crime committed. In the Bible this principle is described as 'an eye for an eye, and a tooth for a tooth'.	A sentence proportionate to the crime, e.g. a long prison sentence for rape.
3 Deterrence	To put the offender and others off (or deter them from) committing crimes because they do not want to incur the punishment.	A fine: it is hoped that people will be deterred from committing certain crimes because they do not want to have to pay money to the courts for breaking the law.
4 Reform	To help the offender change so that he or she will no longer want to commit future criminal acts. It aims to show offenders that what they did was wrong.	Community service. Offenders are kept within the community and are able to continue their normal life. The court sets a number of hours during which the offender is given work to do which will be of benefit to society. It is hoped that the offender will realize why they should not break the law.

Christians do not believe that criminals should not be punished by the State. It is the aims behind the punishment that concern Christians. Generally, Christians agree that society needs to be protected from an offender's criminal activities. Most Christians believe that society needs to deter people from committing crimes; they also believe that the most important aim of any punishment is to reform the offender and not to seek revenge. They would want the punishment to show society's disapproval of the crime while seeking to give offenders the chance to change their ways.

Topic 2 Punishment in practice

The Incident of the Woman Caught in Adultery (John 8:2–11)

At dawn Jesus appeared again in the temple courts, where all the people gathered around him, and he sat down to teach them. The teachers of the law and the Pharisees brought in a woman caught in adultery. They made her stand before the group and said to Jesus, "Teacher, this woman was caught in the act of adultery. In the Law Moses commanded us to stone such women. Now what do you say?" They were using this question as a trap, in order to have a basis for accusing him.

But Jesus bent down and started to write on the ground with his finger. When they kept on questioning him, he straightened up and said to them, "If any one of you is without sin, let him be the first to throw a stone at her." Again he stooped down and wrote on the ground.

At this, those who heard began to go away one at a time, the older ones first, until only Jesus was left, with the woman still standing there. Jesus

straightened up and asked her, "Woman, where are they? Has no one condemned you?"

"No one, sir," she said.

"Then neither do I condemn you," Jesus declared. "Go now and leave your life of sin."

What is...?

An **incident** is an event that actually happened.

Jesus does not deny the Jewish law that the punishment for adultery was death by stoning. He merely says that anyone free from sin may throw the first stone. Only God was considered to be perfect; therefore no one dared to throw a stone, as they would have been guilty of blasphemy. Jesus was left alone with the woman. He refused to condemn her and told her to reform.

Questions

1 What is an incident?
2 What is adultery?
3 **a** Why did the Jews consider adultery wrong?
   b What does this incident tell us about Jesus' teaching on doing wrong and forgiveness?
4 Which line in the Lord's Prayer teaches about forgiveness? Explain what it means.
5 What do you think the incident of the woman caught in adultery and the line in the Lord's Prayer are teaching Christians about the way in which they should treat people who do wrong?

The Incident of the Penitent Thief (Luke 23:32–43)

Two other men, both criminals, were also led out with him to be executed. When they came to the place called the Skull, there they crucified him, along with the criminals – one on his right, the other on his left. Jesus said, "Father, forgive them, for they do not know what they are doing." And they divided up his clothes by casting lots.

The people stood watching, and the rulers even sneered at him. They said, "He saved others; let him save himself if he is the Christ of God, the Chosen One."

The soldiers also came up and mocked him. They offered him wine vinegar and said, "If you are the king of the Jews, save yourself."

There was a written notice above him, which read: THIS IS THE KING OF THE JEWS.

One of the criminals who hung there hurled insults at him: "Aren't you the Christ? Save yourself and us!"

But the other criminal rebuked him. "Don't you fear God," he said, "since you are under the same sentence? We are punished justly, for we are getting what our deeds deserve. But this man has done nothing wrong."

Then he said, "Jesus, remember me when you come into your kingdom."

Jesus answered him, "I tell you the truth, today you will be with me in paradise."

One of the thieves is sorry (**penitent**) for what he has done. He recognizes Jesus as the Messiah, and asks that Jesus remember him. Jesus answers that he will enter heaven with him. The man is dying but God can still forgive him.

This incident suggests that it is never too late to turn back to God. The criminal recognizes Jesus' power to save him from the punishment he deserves for his sins.

? Questions

1 Imagine you are a reporter sent by the local paper to cover the crucifixion of Jesus. Write a newspaper account of the incident of the penitent thief for that evening's edition of the newspaper. Try to include some of your thoughts, feelings and reactions to what you have seen and heard.

2 a Explain the aims of punishment which stoning to death and crucifixion were both trying to achieve.

   b Do you think that these punishments were successful in achieving these aims? Explain your answer.

3 Do you think that most Christians will agree with stoning to death and crucifixion as punishments? Explain the reasons for your opinion, and show that you have thought about more than one point of view.

Topic 3 Stories about forgiveness

What Is ...?

A **parable** is a story. It uses everyday situations to teach people about an idea or a belief.

Jesus used **parables** to teach his followers about forgiveness. Here are two of these parables, the parable of the lost son (or prodigal son) and the parable of the unmerciful servant.

The Parable of the Lost Son (Prodigal Son) (Luke 15:11–32)

Jesus continued: "There was a man who had two sons. The younger one said to his father, 'Father, give me my share of the estate.' So he divided his property between them.

"Not long after that, the younger son got together all he had, set off for a distant country and there squandered his wealth in wild living. After he had spent everything, there was a severe famine in that whole country, and he began to be in need. So he went and hired himself out to a citizen of that country, who sent him to his fields to feed pigs. He longed to fill his stomach with the pods that the pigs were eating, but no one gave him anything.

"When he came to his senses, he said, 'How many of my father's hired men have food to spare, and here I am starving to death! I will set out and go back to my father and say to him: Father, I have sinned against heaven and against you. I am no longer worthy to be called your son; make me like one of your hired men.' So he got up and went to his father.

"But while he was still a long way off, his father saw him and was filled with compassion for him; he ran to his son, threw his arms around him and kissed him.

"The son said to him, 'Father, I have sinned against heaven and against you. I am no longer worthy to be called your son.'

"But the father said to his servants, 'Quick! Bring the best robe and put it on him. Put a ring on his finger and sandals on his feet. Bring the fattened calf and kill it. Let's have a feast and celebrate. For this son of mine was dead and is alive again; he was lost and is found.' So they began to celebrate.

"Meanwhile, the older son was in the field. When he came near the house, he heard music and dancing. So he called one of the servants and asked him what was going on. 'Your brother has come,' he replied, 'and your father has killed the fattened calf because he has him back safe and sound.'

"The older brother became angry and refused to go in. So his father went out and pleaded with him. But he answered his father, 'Look! All these years I've been slaving for you and never disobeyed your orders. Yet you never gave me even a young goat so I could celebrate with my friends. But when this son of yours who has squandered your property with prostitutes comes home, you kill the fattened calf for him!'

" 'My son,' the father said, 'you are always with me, and everything I have is yours. But we had to celebrate and be glad, because this brother of yours was dead and is alive again; he was lost and is found.' "

You need to understand that Jews considered pigs spiritually unclean. This was because God had forbidden Jews to eat pork. The son ended up working with pigs, which shows how low he had sunk since he left home. He even considered eating the pigs' food. Neither son pleased their father, as the older son refused to welcome his brother home. He thought he deserved a reward, as he had always done as his father wished. By not welcoming his brother home, he showed that he was not the loyal son he believed himself to be. The father represents God, and the sons represent ordinary people.

Activity

Using your own words, write out the parable of the lost son in your books.

Can you think of any modern day situations in which people may behave in a similar way?

Questions

1 Why is the son described as prodigal or lost?
2 What is this parable teaching about forgiveness and reconciliation?
3 'The older brother has every right to be upset. He was not treated fairly by his father.' Do you agree? Give reasons for your answer, showing that you have thought about more than one point of view.

2: Crime and Punishment

The Parable of the Unmerciful Servant (Matthew 18:23–35)

Therefore, the kingdom of heaven is like a king who wanted to settle accounts with his servants. As he began the settlement, a man who owed him ten thousand talents was brought to him. Since he was not able to pay, the master ordered that he and his wife and his children and all that he had be sold to repay the debt.

The servant fell on his knees before him. "Be patient with me," he begged, "and I will pay back everything." The servant's master took pity on him, cancelled the debt and let him go.

But when that servant went out, he found one of his fellow servants who owed him a hundred denarii. He grabbed him and began to choke him. "Pay back what you owe me!" he demanded.

His fellow servant fell to his knees and begged him, "Be patient with me, and I will pay you back."

But he refused. Instead, he went off and had the man thrown into prison until he could pay the debt. When the other servants saw what had happened, they were greatly distressed and went and told their master everything that had happened.

Then the master called the servant in. "You wicked servant," he said, "I cancelled all that debt of yours because you begged me to. Shouldn't you have had mercy on your fellow servant just as I had on you?" In anger his master turned him over to the jailers to be tortured, until he should pay back all he owed.

This is how my heavenly Father will treat each of you unless you forgive your brother from your heart.

The servant owed the master a large sum of money ('talents' were coins). The master was willing to cancel the debt when asked. A fellow servant owed this servant a smaller sum. The amount was equal to only a day's wages, but he would not show the same compassion as his master showed. His master was angry and had him severely punished.

The usual understanding of this parable by Christians is that the master (God) is willing to welcome back sinners if they turn to him. People must show God that they are sorry for their **sins**. If God can forgive so much then people must show the same willingness to forgive others.

What is ...?

People who believe in God use the word **sin**. It means an action which goes against God's laws, or which separates people from God.

Questions

1 What is the difference between a parable and an incident?
2 What does the parable of the unmerciful servant teach us about forgiveness?
3 Explain why it is so difficult to show forgiveness to people who have harmed either you or members of your family.
4 Explain how Christians might apply Jesus' teaching in the parable of the prodigal son and the parable of the unmerciful servant to the treatment of offenders and ex-offenders.
5 'Having a Christian faith helps you not to become a criminal.' Do you agree? Show that you have thought about more than one point of view in your answer.

Capital punishment

Capital punishment is the death penalty.

Britain ended the use of capital punishment in 1965. There have been arguments about the death penalty being re-introduced in this country since its abolition. People are divided over the issue of **capital punishment** because it is possible to find biblical teaching to support both points of view.

Arguments in favour of capital punishment

- The death penalty acts as a deterrent to murder. Since its abolition, the number of murders and violent crimes has increased significantly.
- The death penalty protects society. It discourages offenders from carrying weapons for fear of using them in the heat of the moment.
- The death penalty removes the risk of the murderer repeating the crime. There have been murderers who have repeated their crime when freed from prison.
- The death penalty saves money, as society does not have to pay for the offender's upkeep in prison. The money could be used to help those in need.
- Some people regard the death sentence as more humane than a life sentence. There are murderers who have requested it (e.g. Gary Gilmore in the USA requested that he be executed as he did not want to spend the rest of his life in prison).
- The death penalty is the only punishment that reflects society's horror at certain types of crime. This seems to be supported by the book of Genesis, which states: 'Whoever sheds the blood of a man, by man shall his blood be shed; for God made man in his own image.'
- The death penalty agrees with the right of revenge given by Moses: 'an eye for an eye, a tooth for a tooth, a life for a life'.

Arguments against capital punishment

- Other people interpret Moses' words to mean that offenders should pay for the value of the life taken, not have their life taken in return. Jesus taught that people should try to reform the offender, not seek revenge.
- Execution is a barbaric and outdated practice in modern society. The abolition of the death penalty shows progress towards a civilized society.
- The sixth commandment orders people not to kill; yet society would employ a paid executioner if the death penalty were re-introduced.
- St Paul taught that revenge must be left to God. It is for God to seek vengeance, not humans.
- A mistake could be made, and an innocent person executed for a crime he or she did not commit. There is evidence that this has happened in the past.

- The death penalty punishes not only offenders but also their families, because they lose a loved one.
- The death penalty would not stop terrorism. By their actions terrorists have demonstrated that they are not afraid of dying for their cause. They may welcome the opportunity to become martyrs to the cause.

Christians believe that God will forgive the sins of people who are sorry and turn back to him. They believe that they must offer forgiveness to offenders and help them to reform. Nevertheless, society must protect the innocent, and punish crimes. Some Christians say that you should hate the sin but love the sinner. Many Christians believe that punishments must, in the end, help people to reform and become the person God intended that person to be.

Public execution was intended as a deterrent

What do you think?

1 Look back at the incidents and parables of Jesus in this topic.
2 Read again the reasons for and against the death penalty.
3 Imagine that there is to be a debate in Parliament to decide whether the death penalty should be re-introduced for murder. Write the speech that might be given by (i) a Christian MP who supports the re-introduction of the death penalty; and (ii) a Christian MP who is against the re-introduction of the death penalty.

Do you understand...

the Christian attitude to crime and punishment?

Task 1

Look at the picture below.

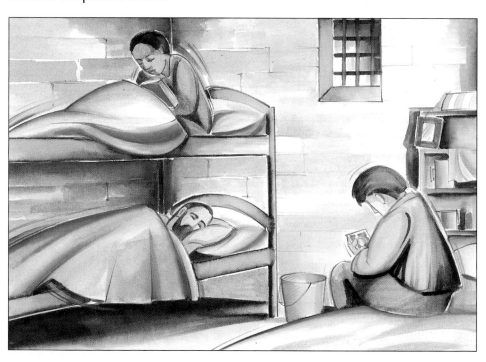

1 State all the aims of punishment. Which of these aims does prison meet?
2 Why do people believe that offenders have to be punished?
3 Look again at the picture. Why do you think that a Christian might feel that the aim of reform is not being met for these prisoners?
4 The majority of prisoners are serving a second or third sentence. Does it seem that prison is successful at reforming offenders? Give evidence from the picture to support your case.

Task 2

1 Find out about the organization NACRO (National Association for the Care and Resettlement of Offenders).
2 Design a leaflet to inform the public about the organization's work.
3 How could an offender be helped:
   a while the offender is still in prison;
   b when the offender leaves prison?
4 Why do Christians feel that they should be involved in helping offenders?

Task 3

Look at the picture below

Would this punishment
stop vandalism?

1 Which aim was this punishment seeking to achieve?
2 **a** Outline an incident when Jesus met a law-breaker.
   b Why might a Christian not agree with the aim of the punishment given
        to the law-breaker in the incident you have chosen?
3 'The re-introduction of the stocks for vandalism would stop it from
   happening.' Do you think most Christians would agree with this
   statement? Support your answer with reference to biblical teaching.

Task 4

1 State **three** reasons which a Christian might give to support the
   re-introduction of the death penalty for murder.
2 State **three** reasons which a Christian might give to oppose the
   re-introduction of the death penalty for murder.
3 State which view you support and give your reasons.

Task 5

1 What is a parable?
2 **a** Outline a parable that teaches forgiveness.
   b What is this parable teaching about forgiveness?
3 A father forgave the drunk driver who knocked down and killed his
   eight-year-old son.
   a Why might some Christians agree with the father's action?
   b Why do many people find it difficult to forgive people who harm
        members of their family? Give reasons for your answer and show
        that you have thought about more than one point of view.

Task 6

1 'Moses taught "an eye for an eye, a tooth for a tooth and a life for a life".
   It is only by making the punishment fit the crime that you will stop the
   increase in offences in Britain.' Do you agree with this statement? Give
   reasons for your opinion and show that you have thought about more
   than one point of view.
2 In the Sermon on the Mount, Jesus taught his followers not to seek
   revenge. Do you think this means that most Christians would not agree
   with Moses' teaching of 'an eye for an eye'? Give reasons for your opinion
   and show that you have thought about more than one point of view.

Topic 1

Conflict

Riots

What is…?

A **riot** is a civil disturbance which results in violent conflict. It is what happens when a group of people 'disturbs the peace' by lawless conduct or behaviour.

What causes people to riot?

There are many causes of **riots.** They could include the following situations:

- One group feels that it receives unfair treatment because of their race or colour.
- In an area of poor housing or high unemployment, feelings of frustration explode into a violent protest.
- A disagreement between two opposing religious or political groups could develop into a violent conflict.

Why do people go to war?

Types of war

There are many different types of war.

A **conventional war** is a war fought between large, uniformed armies, usually from different countries. The armies use conventional weapons such as rifles, machine guns, tanks, aeroplanes and warships. Both armies are trained fighting forces.

A **civil war** takes place within one country. It is what happens when people of the same nation fight each other.

Guerrilla warfare is another form of war that takes place within one country. The guerrillas form an unofficial army who use 'hit and run' tactics against the government's forces. The guerrillas may be untrained. They often rely on the local population to provide their food and weapons, and to hide them from the enemy. These 'unofficial' armed forces are usually trying to change the politics or religion within the country.

Terrorism is war waged by a group against a political or religious system. The terrorists use bombs, kidnapping, hijackings and shooting to fight for their cause. Terrorists often claim that they are forced to act as they do, because it is the only way to remove what they see as an evil political or religious system. An act of terrorism is not open warfare. It may be confined to one nation, or be world-wide.

Chemical and biological warfare seek to gain victory by maiming or killing the enemy. Chemical warfare involves the use of chemicals such as mustard or nerve gas. Biological (germ) warfare involves the use of living organisms such as bacteria or viruses. Both chemical and biological warfare are banned by international agreement, although there is evidence that some countries have continued to experiment with these forms of warfare.

 **What is ...?**

A **war** is an armed conflict between two opposing forces.

Activity

Make a list of the possible causes of a country going to war.

Activity

1 Write the definitions of the different types of war in your book and give an example of an actual war for each type.
2 Briefly investigate a 20th-century war.
3 Write an outline of the war you have chosen. Include in your outline:
   a the names of the countries at war;
   b the cause of the war;
   c how the war began;
   d how the war progressed;
   e how the war ended;
   f what was the outcome or the result of the war.

Nuclear war

What is ...?

Nuclear warfare is the use of nuclear weapons, which kill not only by the immediate impact and heat from the nuclear explosion but also through the long-term effects of radiation sickness.

The first atomic bomb was dropped on Hiroshima, Japan, on 6 August 1945

The USA dropped the only atomic bombs used in a war on the Japanese cities of Hiroshima and Nagasaki in August 1945, towards the end of the Second World War. The two bombs killed hundreds of thousands of civilians. The USA claimed that it used the bombs to bring the end of the war nearer and to avoid further casualties.

Countries have continued to make bigger and more destructive nuclear weapons. There is still a fear that these weapons could be used in a war. Many Western countries have signed a test ban treaty to prevent the testing of nuclear weapons. This has slowed down their development. Recently, however, Asian countries have begun nuclear testing and now have nuclear weapons.

The organisation CND (Campaign for Nuclear Disarmament) wants the destruction of all nuclear weapons. The reasons they give include:

- Nuclear weapons are an unproductive use of the world's resources. The money spent on these weapons of death could be used instead to feed the starving people of the world.
- Countries, such as Japan, which have spent their resources on developing industry instead of building up their stockpile of weapons, have become very successful industrial nations.

- The build-up of arms defeats its objective because tension between the nations increases. War becomes more likely.
- The 1982 report 'The Church and the Bomb' warned that this build-up of weapons increases the risk of innocent lives being lost. In the Book of Proverbs, it states that God hates the shedding of innocent blood.
- The more nuclear weapons there are in the world, the greater is the risk of an accident which could destroy human life.
- Christians support nuclear **disarmament** because Jesus warned that violence leads to violence.
- Nuclear weapons break the commandment 'do not kill' on a massive scale.

NATO (The North Atlantic Treaty Organization) argues that nuclear weapons should be kept. There are Christians who support this view. The reasons they give include:

- Nuclear weapons are an excellent deterrent and stop nations attacking nuclear powers. Nuclear weapons keep the peace because every nation knows that it cannot win a nuclear war; they must therefore find a peaceful solution to disagreements. The existence of nuclear weapons has prevented a third world war.
- A country without nuclear weapons could be held to ransom by nations that are more powerful, or by terrorist groups. A country cannot defend itself against nuclear weapons with conventional weapons.
- The arms trade and nuclear weapons industry is an important part of the world economy, and if the trade ceased many people would lose their jobs.
- If one country launched a nuclear attack against another, it is only right that the other country has the means to retaliate. This would meet the Old Testament demand for 'an eye for an eye'.

What is...?

Disarmament means giving up nuclear weapons.

Unilateral disarmament is when one nation decides to give up its nuclear weapons in the hope that other nations will follow their example.

Multilateral disarmament is when several countries agree to give up their nuclear weapons at the same time.

What do you think?

Could the dropping of a nuclear warhead ever be right?
Give reasons for your view.

Questions

1 a On which country were two nuclear bombs dropped in 1945?
   b What reason did the USA give for the use of these bombs?
2 Write down **two** arguments that some Christians might use in favour of nuclear disarmament.
3 Write down **two** arguments that some Christians might use against nuclear disarmament.
4 Explain the difference between unilateral and multilateral disarmament.

Topic 2 — The arms race

'Mine's bigger than yours'

The arms race between the USSR and the West during the period known as the Cold War (1950s–1980s) led to nuclear weapons being produced in huge numbers. These countries had the nuclear capability to destroy the world many times over. In the 1980s the Soviet President, Mikhail Gorbachev, and the US President, Ronald Reagan, ended the Cold War. They agreed to decrease the stockpiles of nuclear weapons. This, along with the collapse of communism in Eastern Europe, has put an end to the **arms race** between the West and the former USSR.

There is growing concern that money is now being used in developing countries to develop weapons of mass destruction. In developing countries many people live in poverty, and do not have enough food or medical care. Death because of poverty is 33 times more likely in developing countries than death from war. Many people think that such countries need to spend money on health, industrial development and education rather than on bigger and better weapons.

What is ...?

An **arms race** is what happens when one nation improves its military capabilities and other nations believe that they have to do the same.

What do you think?

'Every gun that is made, every warship launched, every rocket fired, signifies in a final sense a theft from those who hunger and are not fed.'
(Dwight D. Eisenhower)

What do you think that President Eisenhower meant when he made this statement?

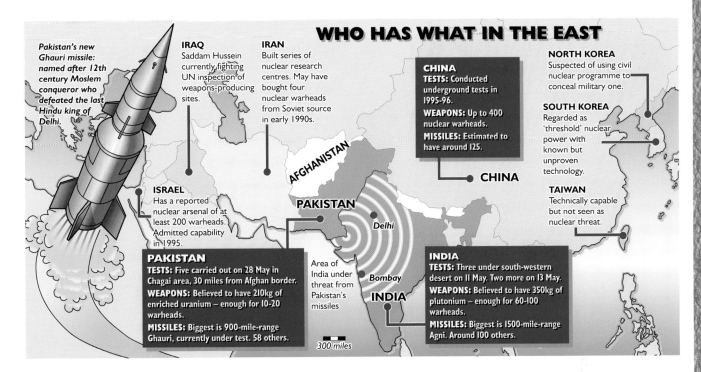

WHO HAS WHAT IN THE EAST

Pakistan's new Ghauri missile: named after 12th century Moslem conqueror who defeated the last Hindu king of Delhi.

IRAQ
Saddam Hussein currently fighting UN inspection of weapons-producing sites.

IRAN
Built series of nuclear research centres. May have bought four nuclear warheads from Soviet source in early 1990s.

CHINA
TESTS: Conducted underground tests in 1995-96.
WEAPONS: Up to 400 nuclear warheads.
MISSILES: Estimated to have around 125.

NORTH KOREA
Suspected of using civil nuclear programme to conceal military one.

SOUTH KOREA
Regarded as 'threshold' nuclear power with known but unproven technology.

TAIWAN
Technically capable but not seen as nuclear threat.

ISRAEL
Has a reported nuclear arsenal of at least 200 warheads. Admitted capability in 1995.

PAKISTAN
TESTS: Five carried out on 28 May in Chagai area, 30 miles from Afghan border.
WEAPONS: Believed to have 210kg of enriched uranium – enough for 10-20 warheads.
MISSILES: Biggest is 900-mile-range Ghauri, currently under test. 58 others.

Area of India under threat from Pakistan's missiles

INDIA
TESTS: Three under south-western desert on 11 May. Two more on 13 May.
WEAPONS: Believed to have 350kg of plutonium – enough for 60-100 warheads.
MISSILES: Biggest is 1500-mile-range Agni. Around 100 others.

300 miles

The Brandt Report stated that the cost of a ten-year programme to solve the problems of developing countries is less than one year's military spending. For example, the cost of one modern jet fighter plane is the same as the inoculation of three million children against the major childhood diseases.

A new arms race began in Asia in May 1998, when India and Pakistan competed with each other for possession of nuclear weapons.

The Middle and Far Eastern arms race

What do you think?

'Disarmament will never succeed.' Do you agree with this statement? Consider the different religious points of view in your answer.

Activity

Study the analysis of the firepower of Middle and Far Eastern countries in May 1998.

Answer the following questions based on it.

1 Why would the countries shown on the map be concerned that their neighbours had entered an arms race?
2 Why do you think that many of the countries on the map did not reveal their nuclear capabilities at the time?
3 Why do you think that:
   a many leaders of Western governments; and
   b many religious leaders are concerned about the growing arms race in the Middle and Far East?
4 How do you think that the Middle and Far Eastern countries would have reacted if other governments had suggested that they sign a test ban treaty? Give reasons for your answer.

Topic 3

Stories about conflict

The Incident of the Cleansing of the Temple (Mark 11:15–18)

On reaching Jerusalem, Jesus entered the temple area and began driving out those who were buying and selling there. He overturned the tables of the money changers and the benches of those selling doves, and would not allow anyone to carry merchandise through the temple courts. And as he taught them, he said, "Is it not written: 'My house will be called a house of prayer for all nations'? But you have made it 'a den of robbers.'"

The chief priests and the teachers of the law heard this and began looking for a way to kill him, for they feared him, because the whole crowd was amazed at his teaching.

The outer court of the temple in Jerusalem was used as a market place. Jews could only pay the temple tax in Jewish coinage, and therefore Jews who had travelled from other countries had to exchange their foreign currency into the Jewish shekel. Jews would buy pigeons or lambs in the market and offer them for sacrifice in the temple. Poor people who came to the temple to worship were being cheated.

Jesus was angry and took the action of driving the traders out of the courtyard. There is no evidence that anyone was physically hurt in the incident, but it was an action which brought Jesus into conflict with the authorities.

In the incident of the cleansing of the temple Jesus is protecting others. He may have been angry that the priests, the very people who should have been helping them, were cheating the poor. Jesus may have disapproved of the use of an important religious building as a market place.

? Questions

1 Where was the temple which Jesus cleansed of traders?
2 Explain why Jesus was angry at what he saw.
3 What do you think Jesus meant by, "'My house will be called a house of prayer for all nations', but you have made it 'a den of robbers'"?
4 Explain how Jesus' action might be applied to conflict with authorities in modern society.

The Incident of the Arrest of Jesus
(Matthew 26:47–53)

While he was still speaking, Judas, one of the Twelve, arrived. With him was a large crowd armed with swords and clubs, sent from the chief priests and the elders of the people. Now the betrayer had arranged a signal with them: "The one I kiss is the man; arrest him." Going at once to Jesus, Judas said, "Greetings, Rabbi!" and kissed him.

Jesus replied, "Friend, do what you came for."

Then the men stepped forward, seized Jesus and arrested him. With that, one of Jesus' companions reached for his sword, drew it out and struck the servant of the high priest, cutting off his ear.

"Put your sword back in its place," Jesus said to him, "for all who draw the sword will die by the sword. Do you think I cannot call on my Father, and he will at once put at my disposal more than twelve legions of angels?"

According to St John's Gospel, the disciple who drew his sword was Peter. Peter was trying to protect his master from his enemies. Jesus stopped him partly because the action might lead to Peter's death, as the group was outnumbered. He may have also believed that using violence was wrong.

The passage suggests that Jesus believed that violence leads to death. If individuals or countries are attacked then they are likely to retaliate. The violence escalates and death results. Many religious people believe that violence is against God's will and is a sin.

 Activity

Write an account of the arrest of Jesus.

What do you think?

'For all who draw the sword will die by the sword.'
How far is this principle a practical guide to living in our time?

Questions

1 Judas Iscariot was a follower of Jesus. What motive(s) might have led Judas to betray Jesus?
2 a How does the incident of Jesus' arrest appear to conflict with the incident of the cleansing of the temple?
  b What can be learnt from both these incidents about Jesus' attitude to the use of violence? Give reasons for your answer.

Topic 4 — Teaching about conflict

What is...?

A **sermon** is a talk. In the Sermon on the Mount, Jesus spoke to the people from the Mount of Olives. He gave a summary of the ways in which he believed people should behave. The sermon includes the teaching of Jesus about how people should obey God and avoid sin.

The Teaching of Jesus on Conflict in the Sermon on the Mount (Matthew 5:38–48)

"You have heard that it was said, 'Eye for eye, and tooth for tooth.' But I tell you, Do not resist an evil person. If someone strikes you on the right cheek, turn to him the other also. And if someone wants to sue you and take your tunic, let him have your cloak as well. If someone forces you to go one mile, go with him two miles. Give to the one who asks you, and do not turn away from the one who wants to borrow from you.

"You have heard that it was said, 'Love your neighbour and hate your enemy.' But I tell you: Love your enemies and pray for those who persecute you, that you may be sons of your Father in heaven. He causes his sun to rise on the evil and the good, and sends rain on the righteous and the unrighteous. If you love those who love you, what reward will you get? Are not even the tax collectors doing that? And if you greet only your brothers, what are you doing more than others? Do not even pagans do that? Be perfect, therefore, as your heavenly Father is perfect."

Jesus is trying to demonstrate how to do more than the minimum to keep the peace and avoid conflict. If people are to live in harmony then situations that lead to conflict should be avoided. Jesus taught that God treats everyone in the same way, whether they are sinners or not. Therefore this is the standard that Christians try to meet.

Questions

1 Look back at the section on the aims of punishment (page 13).
   a Which aim does 'an eye for an eye' meet?
   b Explain what this aim is trying to achieve.
2 Moses said 'an eye for an eye, a tooth for a tooth'.
   a What did Jesus add to this saying?
   b Why do you think Jesus made this addition?
3 State **two** actions that Jesus suggested his followers should do to keep the peace, or to make peace.
4 The passage states that God 'causes his sun to rise on the evil and the good, and sends rain on the righteous and the unrighteous'. What do you think this means?
5 How might a Christian understand the words, 'Be perfect, therefore, as your heavenly Father is perfect.'

St Paul's Teaching on the Authority of the State (Romans 13:1–7)

Everyone must submit himself to the governing authorities, for there is no authority except that which God has established. The authorities that exist have been established by God. Consequently, he who rebels against the authority is rebelling against what God has instituted, and those who do so will bring judgement on themselves. For rulers hold no terror for those who do right, but for those who do wrong. Do you want to be free from fear of the one in authority? Then do what is right and he will commend you. For he is God's servant to do you good. But if you do wrong, be afraid, for he does not bear the sword for nothing. He is God's servant, an agent of wrath to bring punishment on the wrongdoer. Therefore, it is necessary to submit to the authorities, not only because of possible punishment but also because of conscience.

This is also why you pay taxes, for the authorities are God's servants, who give their full time to governing. Give everyone what you owe him: If you owe taxes, pay taxes; if revenue, then revenue; if respect, then respect; if honour, then honour.

St Paul suggests that Christians must obey the ruling authority because God has put the authority there. If the ruler is disobeyed then God is disobeyed. The authority is there for everyone's protection and so there is nothing to fear if one keeps the laws.

St Paul is suggesting that Christians must respect the laws and pay their taxes. If the laws are broken then it is only right that an individual is punished. However, no ruling authority is entitled to ask a Christian to go against their conscience.

 ## What do you think?

Is it ever right to disobey a law? Support your view by describing situations when people may believe protest is the right course of action.

 ## Activity

1 Look up 'St Paul' in an encyclopaedia.
2 It is thought that St Paul was executed on the orders of the emperor Nero. Write St Paul's obituary. (An obituary is a notice in a newspaper of a person's death, with a short biography.)

Questions

1 Why do you think St Paul believed that a ruler must be obeyed?
2 Why do you think that St Paul believed that taxes must be paid?

Topic 5 · Pacifism

What is...?

Pacifists are people who are opposed to using violence and refuse to fight.

Some Christians believe that, however just the cause, war is never the solution. Members of the Society of Friends (Quakers) are Christians who oppose any form of violence. Historically, **pacifists** have been regarded by some people as cowards, and have been punished or rejected for refusing to fight in a war. Some have even been shot for refusing to fight. This happened during the First World War.

Pacifists have proved that they are not cowards. Many pacifists have served in wars under great danger in such non-combatant roles as stretcher-bearers on the front line and ambulance drivers. During a war, pacifists are often called **conscientious objectors**.

Activity

Martin Luther King leads a peaceful protest

The civil rights leader Martin Luther King believed in non-violent protests.

1 Find out the key reasons for the protest led by King in the USA in the 1960s.

2 List as many different forms of non-violent protest that you can think of.

Deitrich Bonhoeffer

Dietrich Bonhoeffer (1906–1945) was a German Lutheran pastor and theologian. The beginning of his ministry coincided with the rise of the Nazi party in Germany. Bonhoeffer first preached pacifism, and non-violent protest against Hitler. When he realized what was happening to German Jews, he helped to organize escape routes for them into Switzerland, and was imprisoned for his activities.

When Bonhoeffer realized that Hitler was not going to listen to peaceful protests, he joined the conspirators working for the overthrow of the Nazi regime. He took part in the failed plot to assassinate Hitler, and was imprisoned in Buchenwald concentration camp. He was executed on 9 April

1945. Bonhoeffer was a pacifist who came to believe that although violence is evil, there are worse evils which can only be dealt with by the use of force.

Martin Luther King remained a pacifist all his life, whereas Deitrich Bonheffer changed his mind and became involved in an assassination plot. Some Christians believe that violence is never right and others that violence is the only way to destroy evil.

Reasons for pacifism

- Jesus taught that violence was wrong and therefore a Christian must abide by this teaching.
- Martin Luther King and Ghandi have proved that it is possible to achieve change without bloodshed.
- Wars never settle disputes. It is only when people have had enough of war and sit down and talk that matters are resolved. It is better to talk in the first place and avoid any loss of life.
- War demoralizes people and the innocent suffer. Pacifism avoids the baser instincts of vice, cruelty and brutality which often emerge during a war.
- The invention of nuclear weapons has resulted in the potential to wipe out the human race. Pacifism would ensure the continuation of the human race.

Reasons against pacifism

- Jesus was not afraid to use force to throw out the traders in the temple. Some Christians believe that this suggests that Jesus was not a pacifist.
- An evil or corrupt ruler would ignore non-violent protests. War may be the only way to remove an evil dictatorship and liberate people.
- If a country has to defend itself against an enemy, then it is only right that all able-bodied members of the country should support the war.
- Wars have brought out some of the best instincts in people: bravery, brotherly love and a willingness to co-operate with others.
- A pacifist nation would be vulnerable to harm from those nations who refuse to give up their weapons.
- The commandment 'Do not kill' refers to murder, not to killing in a just war.

Dietrich Bonhoeffer suffered great hardships in the name of his faith before he was hanged in 1945

What do you think?

'Non-violent protests never work.' Write an essay discussing this statement, showing that you have thought about both sides of the debate before you reached your conclusion.

Questions

1 What is meant by the term 'pacifism'?
2 Why do you think that Quakers are pacifists?
3 What is a conscientious objector?
4 Why do you think that Dietrich Bonhoeffer changed his mind about the use of violence?

Topic 6 · Just and holy war

What is...?

Something which is **just** is believed to be right and fair. It is an action which is thought to have a good reason for it.

Most Christians believe that war should be avoided if possible. Some Christians argue that war is the lesser of two evils. There may be a worse evil, which only a war can defeat. For example, the Second World War was believed to be necessary to remove the Nazi regime.

Christians have disagreed over the correct attitude to war, and how to interpret the teaching of Jesus on the use of violence. Christian pacifists have refused to support any war. Other Christians believe that under certain carefully defined circumstances war is allowed. Such wars are called '**just** wars'.

A just war

War is always a tragedy, but according to the just war theory it is sometimes necessary in order to pursue justice. The just war theory seeks not only to justify certain wars but also to limit war. The theory was first established by St Thomas Aquinas.

St Thomas Aquinas was a 13th-century monk and philosopher. He drew up the theory of a just war to help Christians know whether war was the right action to take. He laid down several conditions for a war to be called just, and other conditions have been added to his original list. The conditions for a just war may be summarized as follows:

St Aquinas laid down the rules of a just war in the 13th century

1 A just war can only be waged as a last resort. All non-violent options must have been tried before the use of force can be justified.

2 A war is just only if a legitimate ruling authority wages it. Even just causes cannot be served by actions taken by individuals or groups who do not have the support of the state or ruler.

3 A just war can only be fought to promote good and overcome an evil. For example, self-defence against an armed attack is always considered a just cause.

4 A war can only be just if it is fought with a reasonable chance of winning, and the minimum amount of force must be used to gain victory.

5 The ultimate goal of a just war is to re-establish peace. Peace must be made as soon as victory is gained.

6 Innocent civilians are never permissible targets of war, and every effort must be taken to avoid killing civilians.

What do you think?

Could a nuclear war ever be a just war? Give reasons for your view and refer to the conditions for a just war in your answer.

Activity

List the conditions for a just war. Think of an example of each one to show that you understand them.

A holy war

The Crusaders believed that they were fighting for God

The early Christians believed in non-violence and did not retaliate when persecuted. They obeyed Jesus' teaching to 'turn the other cheek'. Later some Christians developed the idea that at times God's cause has to be defended. This is a **holy war**, a war fought on behalf of God and supported by God.

The Crusades in the Middle Ages are an example of a holy war. The Christians believed that they were 'rescuing' the holy places in Jerusalem on behalf of God. The word 'crusade' comes from the Latin word for 'cross', and the Crusaders wore a red cloth cross sewn on to their tunics to show people that they were soldiers of Christ.

Questions

1 Explain the differences between a 'just' and a 'holy' war.
2 Describe four conditions that make a war a just war.
3 Some terrorists believe that they are fighting a just war. Is it possible for a terrorist to fight a just war? Support your answer with reference to the conditions required for a war to be just.
4 Can there be a situation, as in a holy war, where God is on one side? Show that you have thought about more than one point of view in your answer.

Do you understand...

the Christian attitude to war and peace?

Task 1

July 1996 in Derry,
Northern Ireland

Look at the picture above and answer the following questions.

1 What might be the cause(s) of the riot shown in the picture?
2 Why would St Paul believe that the riot was the wrong way to protest?
3 Why would a protest led by Martin Luther King not have resulted in a riot?
4 Which saying of Jesus did Martin Luther King instruct his followers to obey?

Task 2

In the last days the mountain of the Lord's temple will be established as chief among the mountains; it will be raised above the hills, and peoples will stream to it. Many nations will come and say, "Come, let us go up to the mountain of the Lord, to the house of the God of Jacob. He will teach us his ways, so that we may walk in his paths." The law will go out from Zion, the word of the Lord from Jerusalem.

He will judge between many peoples and will settle disputes for strong nations far and wide. They will beat their swords into ploughshares and their spears into pruning hooks. Nation will not take up sword against nation, nor will they train for war anymore. Every man will sit under his own vine and under his own fig tree, and no one will make them afraid, for the Lord Almighty has spoken.

(Micah 4:1–4)

The passage is describing a time when there will be unity in the world, and all will follow God's ways. It will be a time of peace and love, when everyone lives in harmony. People will not need weapons of war any longer.

1 The passage suggests that if God's ways are followed there will be no need for war. How do you think that this teaching from the Old Testament is similar to the teaching of Jesus in the New Testament?
2 People are no longer going to fight; they therefore turn their weapons into tools. This would mean the end of the arms race. How would turning weapons into 'ploughshares and pruning hooks' be a better use for the metals in poorer countries?
3 Do you think that there can ever be a time when the whole world lives in peace? Give reasons for your answer, showing that you have thought about more than one point of view.

Task 3

1 Outline the incident of the cleansing of the temple in Jerusalem.
2 Explain how the incident you have described seems to conflict with Jesus' teaching in the Sermon on the Mount.
3 Do you think the teaching of St Paul supports Jesus' action in the incident you have described? Support your answer with reference to St Paul's teaching.
4 Christians are taught to forgive and to 'turn the other cheek'. Explain a situation in which **either** you would find it impossible to 'turn the other cheek' **or** why you would be willing to forgive whatever a person has done.

Task 4

'Does the panel think that Britain should abandon all nuclear weapons to encourage other countries to follow her example?'

Imagine that a member of the audience in the television programme *Question Time* has asked the panel this question. The panel consists of a Christian member of CND, an MP who supports NATO, a Quaker and a nuclear scientist. There is a chairperson to keep order.

1 Write out the answer that you think each member of the panel would give to the question.
2 In groups, present a version of *Question Time* in which the panel answers the above question.

Task 5

1 Look back at the details of the 20th-century war you researched.
2 Explain whether the war you outlined meets the demands of a just war.
3 Do you think that the war you outlined may be described as a holy war? Give reasons for your view.
4 'Greater love has no one than this, that he lay down his life for his friends' (John 15:13). Do you agree with this statement? Give your reasons and show that you thought about more than one point of view before you came to your conclusion.

Topic 1

God's creation

'God looked at everything he had made, and he was very pleased'

The first book of the Bible is **Genesis**. The word 'genesis' means origin. Genesis contains an account of the creation (origin) of the universe by God. In the Genesis story, God created the universe out of nothing. This is followed by the creation of the earth, the creation of all kinds of plants and trees on the earth, and the creation of creatures in the sea, birds in the air and animals on the land. The final life form to appear was human beings. The writer of Genesis states that when God had finished, he looked at everything he had made and he was pleased with it.

Christians believe that God placed humankind in charge of his creation. Genesis states that humankind was given **dominion** over the world. In today's world, Christians understand this to mean that God's creation is on loan to people. Humans are **stewards** of the world, who will one day have to account to their master (God) for the way in which they have treated his property.

What is ...?

Dominion means to have authority over something.

Stewards are in charge of something, such as an estate, on behalf of the owner.

Activity

1 Read Genesis chapter 1.
2 Draw a series of cartoons to show what happened on each day of creation.

What do you think?

'We strive to be good stewards of all the resources entrusted to us, openly accountable for our work.'

(a statement by CAFOD, the official aid and development agency of the Catholic Church in England and Wales)

1 Why do you think the members of CAFOD believe that it is their duty to be 'good stewards'? Explain your answer.
2 Do you think that other Christians would agree with this aim of CAFOD? Explain you answer with reference to the Genesis account of creation.

The environment and pollution

The **environment** may be just the area around a person's home, or it could mean the whole world. There is growing concern at the damage humans are doing to the environment. This damage includes the continual destruction of the rainforests, the hunting of animals to extinction and the **pollution** of both the waters of the earth and the atmosphere above it.

Pollution is not a new problem. In the nineteenth century, during the Industrial Revolution, smoke from factories polluted the atmosphere of cities. The problem is that industry now produces waste that is more damaging to the environment than smoke alone.

What is ...?

The **environment** is the area in which people live. The term also refers to the whole world.

Pollution is the spoiling of the environment through contamination by waste products, such as harmful chemicals and nuclear waste.

Would God look at his creation now and be pleased?

What do you think?

Do you think you live in an area of pollution?

Do you think you have a role to play in stopping the pollution of the environment?

Activity

Industrial waste is not the only way in which humans are destroying the planet.

1 Walk around the school and its grounds, and list all the forms of damage to the environment that you can identify.
2 Discuss and compare your list with the rest of the class.
3 Prepare a report for the headteacher and governors on your findings. Make it clear in your report why you felt that they needed to be informed of your findings.

Questions

1 What do you think that the first chapter of Genesis teaches us about caring for the environment?
2 Explain how people might put the teaching of Genesis into practice in their care of the environment.
3 Explain in your own words the meaning of these terms: dominion; stewardship; environment; pollution.
4 Genesis states that 'God looked at everything he had made, and he was very pleased.' Do you think that God would look at his creation today and be pleased? Give reasons for your answer, showing that you have thought about more than one point of view.

Topic 2

Destroying the planet

Activity

I Look at the images below and list the different forms of pollution you can see.

Pollution destroys the environment

2 In small groups, produce a TV advertisement that is intended to stop one of these forms of pollution.
3 Present your advert to the rest of the class.

Pollution

Pollution is destroying the planet in many ways.

The **greenhouse effect** is caused by the build up of carbon dioxide in the atmosphere, which traps the heat radiated from the earth. This results in a rise in the earth's temperature (**global warming**). Some scientists believe that the long-term effect is extreme weather conditions. The worst consequence of global warming could be the melting of the ice caps at both poles. If the sea levels should rise, many areas would become flooded, and farming land lost.

The ozone layer above the earth filters the ultraviolet rays of the sun. A hole has appeared in the ozone layer above Antarctica, which is getting bigger each year. In other parts of the world, the layer is very thin. Such a rapid decline in global ozone levels endangers the health of the world's population. Increased ultraviolet radiation increases the risk of skin cancer. The major ozone-depleting chemicals are CFCs and other synthetic chemicals.

Acid rain is caused by some of the harmful chemicals that are present in the air. Some of the chemicals are produced by nature itself, such as by volcanoes. The majority are by-products of industrial processes, such as electricity produced from the burning of fossil fuels like coal and oil. Waste gases from these processes may contain sulphur dioxide (SO_2) and nitrogen oxides (NOx, NO_2). When these gases reach the atmosphere and combine with rain, they convert to sulphuric and nitric acid. The resulting acid rain destroys trees and pollutes rivers.

Industrial waste can take many forms and is a cause of much of the pollution in seas and rivers. The waste may be nuclear waste from power stations, or toxic waste from manufacturing processes. Sewage discharges, farm pesticides and oil are other pollutants of the oceans and rivers. This pollution not only kills fish and other sea creatures but can enter the human food chain.

Smoke from factories in Britain can cause acid rain in Sweden

? Questions

1 Explain the greenhouse effect.
2 Why are scientists concerned that a hole has developed in the ozone layer?
3 Why might some people believe that the ozone layer is evidence that God designed the universe?
4 Explain **three** ways in which the earth is being damaged by pollution.
5 'Each generation has a duty to care for the environment for the sake of their children.' Do you think that Christians or other believers would agree or disagree with this statement? Support your answer with reference to the Genesis account of creation, and show that you have thought about more than one point of view.

Saving the planet

Diminishing resources

Pollution is not the only threat to the planet. Another concern is the exhaustion of the world's resources. Our lifestyle has resulted in the world's resources being used up so quickly that they could run out. The non-renewable resources that are thought to be running out include oil, gas and many minerals. Individuals could help to save natural resources by recycling glass and paper, or turning off gas and electrical appliances when they are not in use. Small actions like this can have a positive effect when repeated by people on a national or global scale.

Deforestation is destroying the environment

Other resources are being used up faster than they can be replaced. This includes trees. Timber has been used for centuries to build furniture, houses and ships, but re-planting ensured that there was no significant reduction in the world's forests. But the rainforests are now disappearing at a rate that could cause them to be destroyed within the next fifty years.

Forests are important to provide:

- fuel and timber;
- a barrier to stop soil erosion by the wind;
- a suitable environment for many forms of animals and plants;
- oxygen through photosynthesis that supports life;
- medicines, as one in four of all medicines come from the rainforests – the loss of these medicines could stop treatments for cancer and leukaemia.

In recent years, forests have been destroyed on a large scale. Logging, bulldozing and burning has cleared land for agriculture, cattle and commercial tree plantations. In the developing world, this is known as **slash and burn.**

The land released for farming by slash and burn is soon over-cultivated or over-grazed, and the soil becomes unsuitable for farming. More land is needed, so another area of the forest is cleared. A region that was once lush green forest becomes an arid desert. Every year an area about one-third of the size of Britain becomes a desert in this way. Other forests are cleared to make way for roads and cities.

What is ...?

Slash and burn is a means of clearing forests quickly to release land for crop growing.

Tree-burning on a large scale releases millions of tons of carbon dioxide (CO_2), and raises the earth's temperature by an estimated $3°C$. Deforestation also means that there are fewer trees to absorb CO_2. The destruction of the rainforests is a significant cause of global warming.

The planet can be saved

Although most people are concerned about what is happening to the planet, many argue that there is nothing they can do to stop pollution. This is a mistaken belief, because every individual could reduce the harm he or she causes to the environment.

An individual could:

- avoid dropping litter, which makes people's immediate environment unpleasant;
- avoid using aerosols which contain CFCs;
- walk or use public transport where possible to reduce the pollution caused by car exhausts;
- avoid the use of chemicals in the garden by using organic gardening methods instead;
- start a compost heap in the garden to recycle organic household waste;
- avoid buying pre-packed goods in plastic or polystyrene containers to encourage shops and industry to stop the use of plastic and polystyrene;
- use less detergent in order to decrease the quantity of chemicals polluting rivers and oceans.

Conservation groups have tried to persuade governments to reduce the destruction of the forests. The organization Friends of the Earth, for example, tries to educate people about conservation problems and how to reduce waste.

 **What is …?**

Conservation is the attempt to preserve the planet and to stop the pollution that is destroying it.

 **What do you think?**

'Conservation has nothing to do with me.'

Write a speech for or against this statement for a class debate.

 Activity

Plan a campaign to persuade people in your area to recycle waste. As part of your campaign:

1 Explain why conservation is necessary.
2 Explain how young people can help to reduce the drain on the world's resources.

 Questions

1 Explain the term 'conservation'.
2 Why are conservation groups seeking to protect the rainforests of the world?
3 Suggest **three** ways in which people could help to conserve natural resources.
4 Give some religious reasons why people might believe that they should support the conservation work of Friends of the Earth.

Topic 4

Animal rights

What is...?

An **ecosystem** is the interconnection and dependence of plants and animals on each other, within a specific environment.

A **habitat** is the natural home of a plant or animal.

Pollution and deforestation have resulted in the damage of **ecosystems**. The fine balance between plants, animals, water, air and soil is disturbed, and one result is a destruction of the natural habitat of wildlife.

The clearing of an area of woodland for a road, housing estate or farming land also upsets the balance of nature. The change in the natural **habitat** of plants and animals has led to the near or total extinction of a number of animals and plants.

Animals in danger

It is estimated that more than half of all the world's plant and animal species are found in the tropical rainforests. The destruction of these forests is leading to the extinction of plants and animals at an alarming rate. It is possible that animals and plants have become extinct before their existence has even been established. This may mean the loss of species that could provide new cures for diseases or new crops to feed the starving people of the world.

These elephants could be killed by poachers for their tusks

Activity

1 In small groups, list all the reasons for and against becoming a vegetarian.
2 Discuss your findings with the rest of the class.

The gentle manatee could soon be extinct in Florida

The destruction of the natural habitat of animals is not the only cause of some species coming close to extinction.

The ivory, skin and fur trades have led to the poaching of many animals. Rhinos and elephants are killed for their tusks in Africa. Chinchillas, seals, tigers and leopards have become endangered species because of the skin and fur trade.

Other animals are killed for food. The blue whale is close to extinction because whales are a popular source of meat and other products in Japan. Large numbers of dolphins drown each year because they become trapped in the nets intended to catch tuna. Overfishing of the seas, as well as pollution from toxic waste, is reducing the world's fish stocks.

The hunting of animals is regarded as sport. In Britain, badger baiting is illegal but it still takes place. The high-powered weapons available to hunters means that the number of animals killed during the hunting season has increased significantly. Other animals are harmed by water sports. For example, the use of speedboats throughout the Florida Everglades has brought the manatee close to extinction. There is a growing concern that some species will survive only in zoos.

 What do you think?

> In the Genesis account of creation, Adam named the animals. In the past, this led some Christians to believe that God had placed animals in the world for their use, with no concern for how they were treated. They were involved in many of the activities listed above. Do you think that the majority of Christians and other believers have changed their view about the role of animals in the world? Explain your answer and show that you have thought about more than one point of view.

Individuals and organizations have set up a variety of conservation projects throughout the world. The aim is to investigate the reasons for the disappearance of wildlife populations and to develop new ways of approaching nature conservation. These may include habitat preservation, establishing conservation areas or pressurizing governments to introduce legislation to protect the environment.

Vivisection is the practice of making surgical operations on living animals for research and experimentation.

Anti-vivisectionists are people who oppose vivisection. They argue that scientific and medical research can be carried out without vivisection.

Animal testing is another use of animals to which many people object. One such form of testing is **cosmetic testing** by cosmetics companies.

Costmetic testing

Animals are used as part of scientific experiments in several ways. One controversial form of experiments on animals is **cosmetic testing**. Many cosmetic companies continue to test their products on animals.

One lipstick test (the LD50 Toxicity Test) involves the force feeding of large quantities of lipstick down the throats of animals. This is to find out how much lipstick is needed before it will poison them to death.

Another test (the Draize Eye Irritancy Test) involves the dripping of shampoos, hairsprays and other cosmetics into the eyes of conscious rabbits. This may result in the swelling, discharge and ulceration of the rabbit's eye.

A third test (the Draize Skin Test) involves the applying of products such as aftershave and deodorant to the shaved skin of rabbits and guinea pigs to assess skin damage.

Some companies produce products without testing them on animals. These firms use products known to be safe and kind to skin. The final testing is carried out on human volunteers.

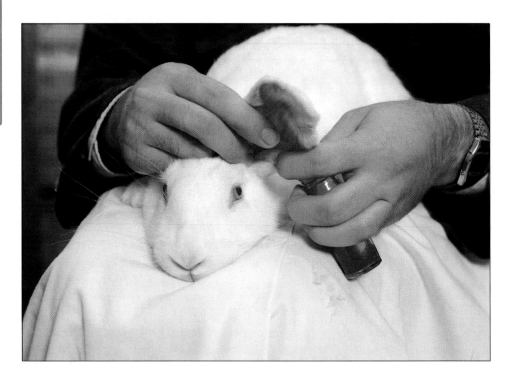

Is it right to test shampoos on rabbits?

Activity

Christians are not agreed that animals have rights. This means that they are divided over the use of animals in scientific experiments.

1 Find out the views of the Roman Catholic, Quaker and one other Christian tradition of your choice, regarding the use of animals in medical and scientific experiments.
2 Write up your findings into a short talk to present to your class.

For and against animal testing

These arguments are put forward by those who support the use of animals in scientific experiments:

- At work safety representatives demand safety data on the substances they handle. These have to be based on animal studies.
- The most significant advances in human health have involved the use of animals. Many of the drugs and operations that save life today would not be in use if it had not been for their original testing on animals.
- The human right to health ultimately takes priority over animal welfare. Faced with a serious illness or a critically ill relative, most people do not hesitate to have their doctors prescribe an effective medicine that will have been thoroughly tested. The original tests probably used animals.
- All responsible medical research involves the use of animals at some stage.
- The public demands increasingly high safety standards for chemicals used in everyday life. People need to be sure that a product will not disfigure or damage them. The only reliable information about the effect of products is available from animal tests.
- The use of animals in research is carefully controlled by law, and abuses are rare. The 1987 Animals (Scientific Procedures) Act says that the project, the researcher and the premises need a licence.

These arguments are put forward by those who oppose the use of animals in scientific experiments:

- Advances in human health owe more to better standards of nutrition and hygiene than to experimental science based on the use of animals.
- There are valid and cheaper alternatives to the use of animals in medical research.
- Animals have the same rights as humans.
- Many of the chemicals used in everyday life are unnecessary and so tests on them cannot be justified.
- Performing animal experiments degrades those who carry them out and should not be permitted. It is not the way God intended mankind to use animals.

 **Questions**

1 What is an ecosystem?
2 List **three** actions that are causing plants and animals to become extinct, and explain how they are causing this.
3 What is vivisection?
4 Give **three** reasons why a Christian may oppose the use of animals in scientific experiments. Support your answer with examples.
5 Give **three** reasons why a Christian may support some use of animals in scientific experiments. Support your answer with examples.
6 'There is nothing wrong with experimenting with animals which have been deliberately bred for that purpose.' Do you agree with this statement? Give reasons for your view.

Topic 5 The Christian response

God created a world in which mankind and animals were to live in harmony

Christians believe that God has provided everything that is needed for survival. The existence of all that is needed to produce life is seen as a proof of God's own existence. There is water, food, air and sunlight to ensure survival of the species. God has not only provided mankind with the necessities of life but has placed humans in a beautiful environment.

Most Christians and other believers think that they not only have a duty to care for the planet but to ensure that the beauty of the planet is preserved to pass on to the next generation. They are therefore concerned that great areas of natural beauty have been spoiled and many species of animal and plants are becoming extinct. Christians believe that they must stop the destruction of the planet and cruelty to animals.

Some Christians believe that it is sufficient to work in their local environment to improve things. Others join local, national or international organizations which seek to improve the environment. One organization they may choose to join is Greenpeace.

Greenpeace

Greenpeace is an international environmental organization founded in 1969 by a group of Canadian environmentalists. The organization uses non-violent, creative confrontation to bring environmental problems to the notice of the rest of the world. The aim is to encourage the introduction of solutions that will preserve the environment for future generations.

Greenpeace states that its goal is 'to ensure the ability of the earth to nurture life in all its diversity'. Therefore Greenpeace seeks to:

- protect biodiversity in all its forms;
- prevent pollution and abuse of the earth's oceans, land and fresh water;
- end all nuclear threats;
- promote peace, global disarmament and non-violence.

Greenpeace monitors the activities of various groups throughout the world. For example, to guard against the extinction of the whale, they monitor the activities of whalers, and make studies of whale populations.

Greenpeace is frequently in the news for its confrontational tactics. Greenpeace protesters often put themselves in danger to protect the environment. In 1985, French agents sank the Greenpeace ship *Rainbow Warrior*, on its way to protest against French nuclear testing.

Members of Greenpeace protesting at the pollution of the seas

 **Activity**

Many Christians become involved with the work of organizations such as Greenpeace.

Imagine you are Canadian Christian who was involved in the founding of the organization. Write a letter to a friend in England explaining why you think that they should join Greenpeace. In your letter explain:

1 why the organization was founded;
2 the aims of Greenpeace;
3 examples of the specific activities of the organization;
4 why you believe that people should be involved with the work of Greenpeace.

 **What do you think?**

Look back at St Paul's teaching in his letter to the Romans (page 33). St Paul said that Christians should obey their ruler. Do you think that St Paul would approve of the work of Greenpeace? Support your points by quoting from St Paul.

Questions

1 'There is nothing I can do to save the whale.' Do you agree with this statement? Give reasons for your answer, showing that you have thought about more than one point of view.
2 What actions could the following people take to help conserve the environment?
   a An individual Christian.
   b A local church group.
   c The world-wide Christian church.
3 If God looked at his creation today he would probably be very puzzled. He would see the splendid achievements of mankind, but he would also see that people and animals are paying a high price for this 'progress'. How could environmentalists explain to God what has happened?

Do you understand...

the Christian view of the environment?

Task 1

> What is man without the beasts? If the beasts were gone, men would die from a great loneliness of spirit. For whatever happens to the beasts, soon happens to man; all things are connected. Whatever befalls the earth befalls the sons of the earth. Man did not weave the web of life, he is merely a strand in it. Whatever he does to the web, he does to himself.
>
> **(Chief Seattle, 1854)**

1 How do the words of Chief Seattle relate to environmental issues?
2 Do you think that much of what he predicted in 1854 has happened? Support your answer with examples.
3 How are the words of Chief Seattle and the creation story in Genesis similar?
4 Chief Seattle was a not a Christian. Do you think that most Christians today would agree with his views? Give reasons for your opinion.

Task 2

> All things bright and beautiful,
> All creatures great and small,
> All things wise and wonderful,
> The Lord God made them all.

1 Do you think some Christians might regard this verse as a suitable reminder of why they should be involved in issues related to animal rights? Give reasons for your answer, showing that you have thought about more than one point of view.
2 Do you think that God made the 'creatures great and small' to be used in scientific experiments? Consider more than one point of view in your answer.

Task 3

1 What do you think the cartoon is trying to say about environmental issues?
2 List **three** ways in which your local environment is being damaged.
3 List **three** ways in which people might try to halt the damage to their local environment.
4 'The environment has got nothing to do with me.' What could be said to such people to change their mind? Support your answer with examples.

Task 4

1 Look again at the account of creation in Genesis.
2 Relate each day of creation to an environmental issue to show how God's creation is being destroyed.

Task 5

Creation in reverse

And the smog and the radio-active material fell on the seas
and the dry land and contaminated every herb yielding
seed and every fruit tree yielding fruit.
And man said:
'It is not very good but we cannot put the clock back.'
This was the fifth day before the end.
And by his work, man created great deserts and changed
climatic conditions so that winds swept the dust of the Earth
skywards to mingle with the smog which blotted out the Sun by
day and the Moon by night so that night and day became the same.
And man saw the work of his hands and said,
'Our conquest of Nature is nearly complete.'
And this was the fourth day before the end.
The third day before the end man said,
'Let us dump our industrial effluents, raw sewage and garbage
into the streams and waterways and seas.'
And it was so.
The waters upon the Earth became foul so that all life in the
waters died.

(From *Beliefs, Values and Traditions*, by Ann Lovelace and Joy White)

1 State **two** ways in which the earth is being damaged in the account above.
2 Explain how the passage above is different from the account of creation in Genesis.
3 Describe one practical way in which a group of Christian teenagers could help to protect the earth.
4 'Christians should be involved in Green issues.' Do you agree? Give reasons for your answer.

Topic 1

The sanctity of life

What is ...?

Sanctity means the quality of being sacred or holy.

When Christians state that life has **sanctity**, they are saying that life is special to God. Each person is a separate, living human being with many rights, especially the right to life. Christian beliefs about God as creator include the belief that all human beings are created as individuals. Every individual is unique, and unlike any other individual in the universe. Human beings have a special place in God's eyes and in God's creation.

> For you created my inmost being; you knit me together in my mother's womb. I praise you because I am fearfully and wonderfully made … My frame was not hidden from you when I was made in the secret place. When I was woven together in the depths of the earth, your eyes saw my unformed body. All the days ordained for me were written in your book before one of them came to be.
>
> (Psalm 139:13–16)

What do you think?

What do you think that this passage from the Old Testament is teaching about the origins of life?

Genesis describes God's creation of the universe. The Bible explains that God's creation of man and woman was personal. Human beings were made in the image, or likeness, of God.

Christians do not agree on how the phrase 'in our image, in our likeness' is to be understood.

Then God said, "Let us make man in our image, in our likeness …" (Genesis 1:26)

What do you think?

What do you think might be the different ways in which the phrase 'in our image, in our likeness' is understood by Christians?

Do you think these different understandings of 'made in God's image' will affect Christian attitudes to the control that they have over life?

> There is a time for everything, and a season for every activity under heaven: a time to be born and a time to die … a time to kill and a time to heal.
>
> (Ecclesiastes 3:1–3)

Christians believe that God is the Lord of life because he is the Creator. God has given life to everyone, so it is only right that he decides when it begins and ends. As life comes from God, then the belief has developed that life itself is sacred – it is holy and set apart for God. This means that life must be protected and used in the way in which God would want.

A question which is often asked is, When does life begin and end?

What do you think?

Do you think a person is alive simply because his or her heart is beating?

Do you think it is right to try to stop a baby being conceived? Support your view with reasons.

Contraception

Roman Catholics believe that life begins at the moment of conception. In Genesis, God said to human beings, 'Be fruitful and increase in number; fill the earth and subdue it.' The Roman Catholic Church teaches that the purpose of sexual intercourse is to reproduce, and therefore to try to stop the conception of a child is a sin; it goes against God's plan. The Roman Catholic Church does not allow the use of artificial methods of birth control. Roman Catholics are only allowed to use natural methods. These include abstaining from sexual intercourse when the woman is most fertile. This is called the rhythm method of contraception.

Most other Christians believe that it is up to each couple to choose whether they want to conceive a child when they have sexual intercourse. These Christians will use artificial methods of contraception, which include the condom, the diaphragm, the pill and the intra-uterine coil. These Christians would argue that God has given human beings intelligence, and they may decide for themselves when it would be best to have a child.

Topic 2

Genetic engineering

Genetics is the science that studies all aspects of inherited characteristics.

Genetic engineering is the application of the knowledge obtained from genetic investigations. Genetic engineering is applied to the solution of such problems as diseases, food production, improvement of a species and infertility.

Scientists believe that **genetic engineering** will bring many benefits to mankind, but many Christians have expressed their concerns about genetic research.

The power of genetic engineering

Genetic engineering could **treat human and animal diseases**. Genetic engineering aims to correct physical birth defects such as Down's syndrome. It may allow scientists to cure medical conditions such as cystic fibrosis, which is the result of a child inheriting a defective gene, or to find a cure for cancer. An example of the way in which gene therapy may be used to cure illnesses was demonstrated by eight-month-old Carly Todd. Carly was born with a fatal immune deficiency disease in 1993. A faulty gene caused the disease. Carly's bone marrow was removed and replaced with marrow with the correct genes added.

Genetic engineering could **overcome the food shortages of the world**. It is used to increase the amount of food available by producing crops that grow faster and bigger, as well as vegetables that have a longer shelf life. Genetically engineered animals exist which can help medical research; they have demonstrated that it is possible to overcome difficulties of cross-breeding between animals. This could result in new breeds of animal, or possibly breeds that could be a better source of protein. In 1997, an identical sheep was 'cloned' from Dolly the sheep. This opens up the possibility of a superstrain of sheep.

The development of **vegetables that are naturally resistant to insects and disease** would reduce the need to use pesticides. The reduction of the use of harmful chemicals would benefit the environment and reduce pollution.

Genetic engineering has given biologists a **greater understanding of the origins of life**. It has become possible to create life outside the womb. The first 'test tube baby', Louise Brown, was born in 1978. There have been significant developments in artificial insemination since that time.

1 Find out the meaning of the terms 'artificial insemination' and 'IVF'.
2 Write an explanation of these terms in your books.

Which forms of genetic engineering do you think that most Christians will accept, and which forms do you think that they will reject as against God's plan? Support your views with biblical and Christian teaching.

The dangers of genetic engineering

There is growing concern that, although genetic engineering may bring advantages, there are dangers as well.

Some people believe that the work of the genetic engineers may be going against God's plan. They fear that scientists are seeking to put themselves in the place of God, when they do not have God's knowledge or wisdom. For example, genetically engineered food could have harmful side effects, which may affect future generations. Genetic engineering could lead to animals that are reared simply to provide spare parts for the human race. Greenpeace is concerned that animals will simply be seen as machines to be treated as people wish. The animals' dignity will be sacrificed for the supposed benefits to humans.

People wonder whether life will be treated as a commodity simply to be traded for money. They are concerned that it will be profit, not human need, which will drive the way in which genetic knowledge is used. Is there a danger that science will go ahead with genetic research and development without understanding the full effects of its actions?

Is genetic engineering interfering with God's plan?

 ## What do you think?

Dolly the sheep

The cloning of Dolly the sheep has raised the possibility that humans could be cloned. Christians believe that each person has a special relationship with God. Do you think that the cloning of human beings would go against the sanctity of human life? Give reasons for your view.

 ## Questions

1 What do you understand by the term 'the sanctity of life'?
2 What is genetic engineering?
3 Give **three** reasons why a Christian might support genetic engineering.
4 Give **three** reasons why a Christian might oppose genetic engineering.
5 Do you think that there should be stricter controls on genetic engineering? Give reasons for your answer.

Topic 3 Abortion

What is …?

An **abortion** is the termination (ending) of a pregnancy before birth, either by natural or artificial means. An abortion is the premature expulsion from the body of an embryo or foetus.

Before abortions were made legal, many women went to 'back-street' abortionists. These were illegal abortions, often performed by untrained people in unhygienic conditions. The result was many women were seriously injured and about 30 women died each year.

In 1967 Parliament passed an Abortion Act, which made an abortion legal if it was performed in the first 28 weeks of the pregnancy. The Human Fertilization and Embryology Act 1990 reduced the time in which a legal termination is permitted to 24 weeks. An abortion is legal if two doctors agree that one of the following circumstances exists:

1 there is risk to the life of the mother if the pregnancy continued; or

2 there is risk of injury to the mental or physical health of the mother; or

3 there is a substantial risk that, if the child were born, it would suffer from physical or mental abnormalities; or

4 there is risk to the physical or mental well being of her existing children if the pregnancy continues.

Activity

I Copy the chart below on to paper.

Reasons for abortion	Reasons against abortion

2 Read the arguments for and against abortion (below).
3 Using your own words, complete the chart.

Arguments in favour of abortion

People who support abortion, such as the Abortion Reform Group, put forward the following arguments in favour of abortion.

• A woman should have the right to choose what happens to her body.
• If it becomes more difficult to get legalized abortions there would be an increase in the number of illegal abortions.
• It is wrong to bring unwanted children into the world, especially if a child is handicapped. Unwanted children may suffer rejection and become problems in society.
• When pregnancy is the result of rape, the woman should not be forced to continue with the pregnancy.
• Abortion is not murder as it destroys only a collection of cells, which cannot survive outside the womb before the 24th week of the pregnancy.
• A woman who is at risk of dying, or of being handicapped, by the pregnancy should be allowed an abortion, especially if she already has children needing her care.

Arguments against abortion

Organizations such as Save the Unborn Child (Life) put forward the following arguments against abortion.

- The unborn child is alive from the moment of conception and has the right to life. An abortion is infanticide (child killing).
- If abortions are easily obtained, they may be used as another form of contraception, thus encouraging people to have a casual attitude to sexual relationships.
- Many couples would welcome the chance to adopt an unwanted baby, but abortions have reduced the number of babies available for adoption.
- There are physical and mental risks for the woman who has an abortion. The operation may lead to sterility. Many women have suffered guilt feelings afterwards, which have resulted in depression and in some cases suicide.
- There would be no need for women to seek abortions if there was sufficient provision to help them overcome any emotional and financial difficulties the pregnancy will cause.

The Christian position on abortion

The Bible does not make any direct reference to abortion. Christians have to decide when life begins before deciding whether or not abortion breaks the commandment not to kill.

Some Christians believe that abortion is murder because an abortion breaks the commandment 'Do not kill'. The Roman Catholic Church believes that life begins at the moment of conception and that everyone has the right to life.

When does life begin?

There are other Christians, such as Anglicans and Methodists, who believe that life does not begin until the baby has a chance of surviving independently of its mother. These Christians believe that an abortion is an evil to be avoided if at all possible. However, abortion could be justifiable if it meant that greater evils were avoided. An abortion could be justifiable if there were a risk to the physical or mental health of the mother, if she were likely to give birth to a handicapped child or if the pregnancy were the result of rape.

The organization Christians for Free Choice believe that the matter should be left to a woman's own conscience; conscience is seen as a guide from God as to what action to take. The decision to continue a pregnancy should not be forced on a woman.

Activity

1 Look back at the section on situation ethics (page 6).
2 A sixteen-year-old girl has become pregnant after she was raped. Write a paragraph as a supporter of situation ethics in response to the statement, 'The most loving thing is for her to be allowed an abortion.'

What do you think?

In class, debate the following statement: 'Abortion should be abolished.'

Topic 4

The parable of the sheep and the goats

Activity

Look back to page 16. What is a parable?

Christians believe that the following parable teaches them what it means to be a Christian.

The Parable of the Sheep and the Goats (Matthew 25:31–46)

When the Son of Man comes in his glory, and all the angels with him, he will sit on his throne in heavenly glory. All the nations will be gathered before him, and he will separate the people one from another as a shepherd separates the sheep from the goats. He will put the sheep on his right and the goats on his left.

Then the King will say to those on his right, "Come, you who are blessed by my Father; take your inheritance, the kingdom prepared for you since the creation of the world. For I was hungry and you gave me something to eat, I was thirsty and you gave me something to drink, I was a stranger and you invited me in, I needed clothes and you clothed me, I was sick and you looked after me, I was in prison and you came to visit me."

Then the righteous will answer him, "Lord, when did we see you hungry and feed you, or thirsty and give you something to drink? When did we see you a stranger and invite you in, or needing clothes and clothe you? When did we see you sick or in prison and go to visit you?"

The King will reply, "I tell you the truth, whatever you did for one of the least of these brothers of mine, you did for me."

Then he will say to those on his left, "Depart from me, you who are cursed, into the eternal fire prepared for the devil and his angels. For I was hungry and you gave me nothing to eat, I was thirsty and you gave me nothing to drink, I was a stranger and you did not invite me in, I needed clothes and you did not clothe me, I was sick and in prison and you did not look after me."

They also will answer, "Lord, when did we see you hungry or thirsty or a stranger or needing clothes or sick or in prison, and did not help you?"

He will reply, "I tell you the truth, whatever you did not do for one of the least of these, you did not do for me."

Then they will go away to eternal punishment, but the righteous to eternal life.

Jesus is teaching here that a Christian must help people in need. If people in need are not helped then the message brought by Jesus is ignored. If the message of Jesus is ignored then people will have separated themselves from God. They will not have gained God's forgiveness for their sins.

The parable teaches Christians to look after people whatever their needs. This is one way in which Christians are expected to follow Jesus' example. Many Christians believe that this includes caring for the disabled: to terminate a life on the grounds of disability is not acceptable in God's eyes. It is not for others to judge the quality of another person's life. It is for a Christian to seek to make that quality of life the best that it can be by helping to care for all the people of the world.

Activity

Find out the different ways in which Christians understand the parable's references to 'eternal punishment' and 'everlasting life'.

Questions

1 Outline the parable of the sheep and the goats.
2 Why are the sheep (the righteous) rewarded for their behaviour?
3 Why are the goats punished for their behaviour?
4 In what ways do you think people might apply the teaching of this parable to the way in which they treat people in need? Support your answer with examples.

Euthanasia

What Is ...?

Euthanasia is the practice of ending the life of people who are suffering from incurable diseases or handicap, using painless methods. The intention of euthanasia is to avoid prolonging their suffering. It is sometimes called mercy killing.

Passive euthanasia is when no action is taken to prolong life, but there is no deliberate action to end the life. For example, if a person dying of cancer has a heart attack there would be no attempt to resuscitate him or her.

Active euthanasia is when a deliberate action is taken to end a life, such as the administration of a lethal injection of an overdose of a drug, or the active withdrawal of a life-supporting drug or machine.

What do you think?

Why do you think that some Christians will support passive euthanasia but are opposed to active euthanasia? Support your answer with biblical and Christian teaching.

Arguments in favour of euthanasia

Euthanasia is illegal in England and Wales. The organization EXIT (the Voluntary Euthanasia Society) campaigns for a change in the law to legalize voluntary euthanasia. The organization puts forward the following arguments in favour of euthanasia.

Is life on a machine really life?

- People should be allowed to decide for themselves when they want to die. Suicide is legal, so why not euthanasia?
- Christians accept that life comes from God, but there is nothing in the Bible which states that a person must be kept alive at any cost. Keeping

people alive by machine is not life in the true sense. It is wrong to preserve life beyond its natural span.

- Euthanasia would allow people to die with dignity. The person can die with their family and friends around them in a loving atmosphere, with all their affairs in order.
- Relatives would be spared the risk of watching loved ones suffer a slow, painful death.
- Animals are not allowed to suffer; the same compassion should be shown to humans.

Arguments against euthanasia

Christians opposed to euthanasia put forward the following arguments.

- Christians believe that God gives life and that they are accountable to God. God is the giver of life and therefore only God may end it. 'You are not your own,' St Paul declared (I Corinthians 6:19). 'If we live, we live to the Lord; and if we die, we die to the Lord. So, whether we live or die, we belong to the Lord' (Romans 14:8).
- Christians believe that suffering is a way of strengthening faith and is there for a purpose. It is not for an individual to try to escape from God's plan for them.
- Euthanasia goes against the commandment, 'Do not kill'. Euthanasia is murder.
- God may have plans for people even when it appears that their life is finished. The physicist Professor Stephen Hawking has motor neurone disease. He has written the best-selling book *A Brief History of Time* since he became paralysed.
- Helping the sick, disabled and old teaches compassion. It offers the chance to put Christian teaching into practice. The parable of the sheep and the goats warns that God will judge people on how they have helped those in need.
- The doctor's diagnosis may be wrong. The chance of a cure or miracle is removed if euthanasia takes place. People recover from illnesses and accidents against all expectations.
- The doctor/patient relationship would change. Doctors take the Hippocratic Oath to preserve life. The legalization of euthanasia could cause patients to wonder if the doctor is doing everything possible to cure them.
- The old and disabled might feel that they should accept euthanasia to avoid being a burden to their family or society.
- Many people accept euthanasia because they are afraid of the pain or loss of dignity that might result from a terminal illness. If the correct care is provided, the dying can be given dignity and freedom from pain. The hospice movement provides surroundings in which a dying person's emotional and spiritual needs are met as well as his or her physical needs.

 **Questions**

1 What is euthanasia?
2 Explain the difference between passive and active euthanasia.
3 'Euthanasia should never be legalized in Britain.' Do you agree? Give reasons for your opinion, and show that you have thought about more than one point view.

Do you understand...

the Christian attitude to the sanctity of life?

Task 1

Read the following passage from Luke's Gospel and answer the questions which follow.

> I tell you, my friends, do not be afraid of those who kill the body and after that can do no more. But I will show you whom you should fear: Fear him who, after the killing of the body, has power to throw you into hell. Yes, I tell you, fear him. Are not five sparrows sold for two pennies ? Yet not one of them is forgotten by God. Indeed, the very hairs of your head are all numbered. Don't be afraid; you are worth more than many sparrows.
>
> **(Luke 12:4–7)**

1 Explain this passage in your own words.
2 How does this passage link to the Christian belief in the sanctity of life?
3 Why do you think some Christians use this passage to oppose genetic engineering, abortion and euthanasia?
4 Do you think that this passage would give comfort to a dying person? Give reasons for your answer.

Task 2

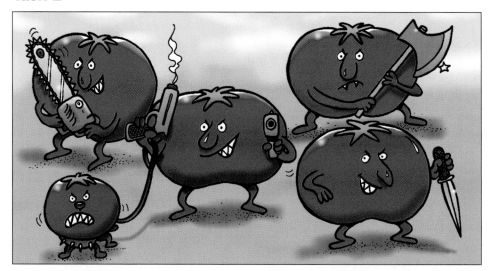

Could we end up with killer tomatoes?

Christians believe that mankind 'is made in the image of God'. What problems do advances in genetic engineering pose for Christians?

Task 3

A very able sixth-form pupil, Lisa, intended to go to university. Two months before her A-level examinations Lisa discovered that she was pregnant. When she told her boyfriend, he told her to 'get rid of it', and wanted nothing more to do with her. Lisa felt that she did not want to continue with the pregnancy as she wanted a career, and a husband, before she started a family. Her mother, as an active member of LIFE, the anti-abortion organization, wanted her daughter to have the baby and to go to the local college. She said that the family could help Lisa to bring up the child while Lisa continued her studies. Lisa's father was a member of the Church of England and attended church regularly. Lisa was surprised when he supported her wish to have an abortion. He said that he would agree with her action if the abortion took place before the pregnancy had developed beyond the twentieth week. Lisa decided to go to a clinic and have her pregnancy terminated. She passed her examinations and is now following a degree course at university.

Both parents in the extract are Christians. The mother supports the anti-abortion campaign, and yet the father supports his daughter's opinion.

1 Explain how Christians who share the father's view would justify allowing an abortion.
2 Explain how Christians who share the mother's view would justify being against abortion.

Task 4

'The Bible commands "Do not kill". Therefore abortion is clearly wrong.'

1 Arguing from Christian as well as other sources, what arguments do you think people would give in support of this statement?
2 Arguing from Christian as well as other sources, what arguments do you think people would give in opposition to this statement?
3 Do you believe that there should be any changes in the abortion law? Give reasons for your view.

Task 5

Pope John Paul II made a statement which condemned both abortion and euthanasia. He stated that they are 'crimes which no human law can claim to legitimize. Abortion always constitutes a grave moral disorder since it is the deliberate killing of an innocent human being.'

Do you think that all Christians would agree with Pope John Paul's view that abortion and euthanasia are crimes? Give reasons for your opinion, showing that you have thought about more than one point of view.

Topic 1 Love and friendship

 What is ...?

Philos means the love that people have for their friends.

Agape is unselfish love. It is the love which seeks to help people in need. Agape is the sort of love to which Christians refer when they talk of the 'love of one's neighbour'.

Eros is the romantic love which a man and woman may have for each other.

 Activity

Write a poem or a description about your idea of a true friend.

A friendship is one of the most important relationships that people can form. A true friend gives support, not only when things are going well but also when things go wrong.

There are many types of friends. There are friends who you meet at school to chat with and share the activities of the school day. There are special friends with whom you not only share activities but also your thoughts and feelings. These are the people who stay as your friends for most of your life. If special friends let you down it is very hurtful.

Jesus had many friends, and he used to go to their homes for meals. He had a group of twelve special friends called the **disciples** or **apostles**. One of these friends betrayed him (Judas Iscariot), and another (Simon Peter) denied that he knew Jesus three times after Jesus was arrested.

 What do you think?

How do you think Jesus felt to be betrayed by one friend and denied by another?

Do you think it is worse to be let down by friends rather than by people you hardly know?

 Activity

Look back to the story of the arrest of Jesus on page 31.

Judas betrayed Jesus using the greeting of a friend. What was this greeting?

The Gospels describe the time that Jesus spent with the disciples after he had risen from the dead. On one occasion he showed Peter that he had forgiven his betrayal (see extract, page 67).

Jesus asked Peter if he loved him. He is talking about Peter loving him as a friend, which is not the same love as he meant people to give to their neighbour. Nor is it the same as the love parents feel for their children, or a man for his wife. The problem is that in English we have only one word for love. In Greek, the language of the New Testament, there are several different words to explain the different forms of love that exist (see box).

The Incident of Peter's Forgiveness (John 21:15–17)

When they had finished eating, Jesus said to Simon Peter, "Simon son of John, do you truly love me more than these?"

"Yes, Lord," he said, "you know that I love you." Jesus said, "Feed my lambs."

Again Jesus said, "Simon son of John, do you truly love me?"

He answered, "Yes, Lord, you know that I love you."

Jesus said, "Take care of my sheep."

The third time he said to him, "Simon son of John, do you love me?"

Peter was hurt because Jesus asked him the third time, "Do you love me?" He said, "Lord, you know all things; you know that I love you."

Jesus said, "Feed my sheep."

 **Questions**

1 Why do you think that Jesus asked Peter three times 'Do you love me?'
2 What do you think Jesus meant when he told Peter to 'Feed my sheep'?
3 What do you think this incident teaches Christians about forgiveness, friendship and love?

Is it possible to love your enemy?

Christians believe that their faith makes them all one family, and that they should love and care for each other. Christians are taught that they must not only love their friends but also their enemies as well.

When children are small, they tend to have friends of the same sex. When they are teenagers, they begin to have friends of both sexes. Sometimes the friendship deepens and changes into a sexual attraction, which goes beyond friendship.

Activity

A new pupil arrives in a school half way through the school year. No one in their class speaks to the pupil or tries to make the pupil feel welcome.

List how it may feel to have no friends.

Topic 2 Christian attitudes to sex

What is …?

Pre-marital sex is sexual intercourse between two people who are not married.

Extra-marital sex is sexual intercourse between a couple when at least one of them is already married to another person.

Many Christians believe that sex outside marriage is not what God wants, and some consider it a sin. **Pre-marital sex** and **extra-marital sex** are two terms used to describe sex outside marriage.

There are several passages in the Bible which suggest that neither form of sexual intercourse is intended by God. St Paul wrote a letter to the people of Corinth in which he made it very clear that he did not agree with sex outside marriage.

Flee from sexual immorality. All other sins a man commits are outside his body, but he who sins sexually sins against his own body. Do you not know that your body is a temple of the Holy Spirit, who is in you, whom you have received from God? You are not your own; you were bought at a price. Therefore honour God with your body.

(1 Corinthians 6:18–20)

'You were bought at a price'

Questions

1 What did St Paul mean by 'sexual immorality'?
2 Why do you think that St Paul believed having sex outside marriage was particularly sinful?
3 Why did St Paul believe that people should keep their bodies as a 'temple of the Holy Spirit'?
4 St Paul wrote, 'You are not your own; you were bought at a price.'
   a What did St Paul mean by the phrase 'you were bought at a price'?
   b Why did he believe this meant that people should refrain from sex outside marriage?

Pre-marital sex has led to an increase in the number of illegitimate babies born each year, and the spread of sexually transmitted diseases. Christians argue that if St Paul's teaching is obeyed there would not be these problems in society.

 ## What do you think?

Does sex eduction encourage young people to have sex outside marriage?

Extra-marital sex is usually called **adultery**. The seventh commandment states that people must not commit adultery. Jesus taught that not only is adultery wrong, but also to look at someone **lustfully** is wrong.

Jesus stated that adultery was wrong in his Sermon on the Mount.

You have heard that it was said, "Do not commit adultery." But I tell you that anyone who looks at a woman lustfully has already committed adultery with her in his heart. If your right eye causes you to sin, gouge it out and throw it away. It is better for you to lose one part of your body than for your whole body to be thrown into hell. And if your right hand causes you to sin, cut it off and throw it away. It is better for you to lose one part of your body than for your whole body to go into hell.

It has been said, "Anyone who divorces his wife must give her a certificate of divorce." But I tell you that anyone who divorces his wife, except for marital unfaithfulness, causes her to become an adulteress, and anyone who marries the divorced woman commits adultery.

(Matthew 5:27–32)

Jesus is warning that lustful thoughts are the motive behind adultery. He is trying to stop people from following a course of action that could lead to sin. When he refers to gouging out an eye, he means that people have to take steps that are painful to stop something worse happening to them. He means it may be difficult to avoid giving in to the temptation to have an affair, but it is better to do that than to end up being punished by God. Hell will be a far worse fate.

 ## Questions

1 Explain why Jesus thought lustful thoughts were equal to adultery.
2 The suggestion that one should gouge out an eye or cut off a hand sounds extreme. Explain what Jesus was trying to teach when he gave these instructions.
3 What did Jesus state a person was guilty of if they divorced and took another partner?

 ## Activity

In groups, list reasons why Christians are concerned about sex outside marriage, especially when it involves young people.

Discuss the list with the rest of the class and then write down the complete list of reasons given by the whole class.

What is ...?

Lust means to have a physical desire for someone.

Topic 3 — Marriage

More than 85 percent of adults marry at some time in their lives. Nearly half the couples who marry have previously lived together before marriage.

Couples have many reasons for marrying. The obvious one is that they are in love and want to make a commitment to each other. Other reasons may be:

- A baby is on the way, and they want the child to have parents who are married.
- A couple will be financially better off, as the man gets a married man's tax allowance.
- It is less confusing if the couple have the same surname.
- It gives both parties security under the law.
- The couple wants to celebrate their love publicly by having a wedding ceremony.

The relationship between a husband and wife changed a great deal in the 20th century. A woman no longer has to agree to obey her husband in the ceremony. Most brides who marry in church wear white. This tradition dates back to the 19th century when it was assumed that a woman would be a virgin on her wedding day. The white dress was introduced as a symbol of her purity. Although many couples live together before marriage and therefore the bride is not necessarily a virgin on her wedding day, the tradition has continued. A couple could wear jeans for a church wedding if they wanted to as there is no set dress code for either a church or a registry office wedding.

Activity

Think about your ideal marriage partner. What do you think are the most important qualities you would be looking for in a husband or wife?

What do you think?

Some people have said that unmarried couples living together are 'living in sin'.

Do you think that living together before marriage separates people from God? Give reasons for your opinion, showing that you have thought about more than one point of view.

Activity

Find out the current requirements necessary to make a marriage legal in England and Wales.

A Teaching of St Paul on Marriage (Ephesians 5:21–33)

Submit to one another out of reverence for Christ.

Wives, submit to your husbands as to the Lord. For the husband is the head of the wife as Christ is the head of the church, his body, of which he is the Saviour. Now as the church submits to Christ, so also wives should submit to their husbands in everything.

Husbands, love your wives, just as Christ loved the church and gave himself up for her to make her holy, cleansing her by the washing with water through the word, and to present her to himself as a radiant church, without stain or wrinkle or any other blemish, but holy and blameless. In this same way, husbands ought to love their wives as their own bodies. He who loves his wife loves himself. After all, no one ever hated his own body, but he feeds and cares for it, just as Christ does the church – for we are members of his body. "For this reason a man will leave his father and mother and be united to his wife, and the two will become one flesh." This is a profound mystery – but I am talking about Christ and the church. However, each one of you also must love his wife as he loves himself, and the wife must respect her husband.

 What do you think?

Does St Paul's attitude to marriage seem outdated in modern society? Give reasons for your view.

St Paul believed that the husband is the head of the household, just as Jesus is head of the Church. A woman must abide by her husband's instructions. A husband must care for his wife and love her as he loves himself. In an Orthodox marriage ceremony the link between Christ and his Church and the husband and wife is remembered by the 'crowning' of the bride and groom.

Jesus and St Paul taught that marriage is for life and adultery is a sin. When the couple marry and have sexual intercourse they become 'one flesh'. Only God may end this bond; the marriage ends when one of the partners dies. The Christian marriage ceremony therefore includes the vow to be faithful for life.

'the two will become one flesh'

 What do you think?

'Women should still vow to obey their husbands in the marriage ceremony.'

Do you agree with this statement? Give reasons for your opinion, showing that you have thought about more than one point of view.

Activity

In pairs, list the things that you believe a couple needs to consider before they marry.

The marriage ceremony

In a Christian marriage ceremony, the couple is left in no doubt as to the meaning of marriage. At the beginning of the ceremony, they are reminded that it is a serious undertaking that is not to be entered lightly. The nature of the relationship between a husband and wife is established as they exchange their vows.

 Activity

The opening of the marriage ceremony in the Church of England (below) states the Christian beliefs about the purpose of marriage. Read it and write out the three purposes of marriage given.

> *It is God's purpose that as husband and wife give themselves to each other in love throughout their lives, they shall be united in that love as Christ is united with his Church. Marriage is given, that husband and wife may comfort and help each other, living faithfully together in need and in plenty, in sorrow and in joy. It is given, that with delight and tenderness, they may know each other in love, and through the joy of their bodily union, may strengthen the unions of their hearts and lives. It is given, that they may have children and be blessed in caring for them, and bringing them up in accordance with God's will, to his praise and glory.*

(Alternative Service Book, 1980)

The following marriage vows may be found in the Alternative Service Book of the Church of England. During the service the vicar will ask the bride and groom in turn:

> *(Name), will you take (Name) to be your husband? Will you love him, comfort him, honour and protect him, and forsaking all others, be faithful to him as long as you both shall live?'*

The bride and groom will agree that:

> *I, (Name), take you, (Name), to be my wife; to have and to hold; from this day forward; for better, for worse, for richer, for poorer, in sickness and in health, to love, and to cherish, till death us do part, according to God's holy law; and this is my solemn vow.*

 Activity

1 Copy out the vows exchanged in a marriage ceremony in the Church of England.
2 Explain in your own words the meaning of the vows that the bride and groom are taking.

Christians believe marriage is for life. This is symbolized by the ring that is exchanged during the marriage ceremony.

> *I give you this ring as a sign of our marriage. With my body I honour you, all that I am I give to you, and all that I have I share with you, within the love of God, Father, Son and Holy Spirit.*

There are several reasons why couples choose a **civil ceremony** rather than a religious ceremony. These include:

The wedding ring symbolizes the bond between a husband and wife

- The couple does not want a religious ceremony, in which vows are taken before God.
- Many couples feel that they cannot take a vow to be faithful for life. A civil ceremony does not require the couple to make such a vow.
- One or both partners have been divorced, so some Christian denominations will not allow them to remarry in church.
- The couple may be of different faiths, and cannot agree on a religious ceremony.

In a civil ceremony the only words the couple need to say to each other by law are:

> *I (Name) hereby solemnly declare that I know of no legal impediment to my marrying (Name).*
>
> *I call upon these persons here present to witness that I (Name) do take thee (Name) to be my lawful wedded husband/wife.*

What do you think?

Do you think the vows in a civil ceremony are appropriate for a modern marriage, or do you think they are too short?

Activity

1 Write your own marriage vows for a civil ceremony.
2 Explain the reasons for the differences you have chosen to make between your vows and those made by a Christian in the Church of England marriage ceremony.

Questions

1 Give **three** reasons why a couple may choose a civil rather than a religious ceremony.
2 Explain why a Christian couple may wish to marry in a church rather than a registry office.
3 State **three** major differences between a civil and a religious marriage ceremony.
4 Explain how the marriage vows in a Church of England ceremony reflect a Christian view of marriage.

Topic 4 Divorce

'What God hath joined together, let no man put asunder'

What is...?

A **divorce** is the legal termination of a marriage. After a divorce, the couple is free to remarry.

Many couples who have agreed to marry 'until death us do part' find that they can no longer live together, and end their marriage by **divorce**.

Activity

1 In small groups, make a list of the causes of stress in a marriage.
2 Report the list back to your teacher for a class list to be made.
3 Write down the complete list.

The divorce laws

The Divorce Reform Act 1971 makes the only ground for divorce the 'irretrievable breakdown' of the marriage. For a divorce to be allowed, the couple has to provide proof that the marriage has irretrievably broken down. The courts, as proof of this 'irretrievable breakdown', accept one of the five reasons below:

- If one partner has committed adultery.
- If one partner has treated the other unreasonably, either by physical or mental cruelty or insanity.
- If one partner has been deserted by the other for a continuous period of two years.
- If the partners have lived apart for two years, and both consent to a divorce.
- If the partners have lived apart for five years, but only one partner will consent to a divorce.

Activity

Look again at St Paul's teaching in Ephesians (page 71). Does this passage have any implications for the Christian view of divorce?

The 1984 Matrimonial and Family Proceedings Act allows a couple to seek a divorce after only one year of marriage, rather than the three years that couples previously had to wait.

Christian attitudes to divorce

Christians take a vow in the marriage ceremony to be together 'till death us do part'. Christians agree that divorce is not what God wants and should be avoided. Some Christians, however, find that they cannot cope with their marriage, so they divorce. The major Christian denominations are divided on whether a divorced couple should be allowed to marry again, and whether the second marriage ceremony may be in church.

The **Roman Catholic Church** does not accept divorce. In the eyes of this denomination, the couple is married for life, and therefore to remarry would be adultery. Occasionally an **annulment** is allowed if, for example, there has never been sexual intercourse between the couple.

The **Church of England** does not, in principle, accept divorce. The church teaches that marriage is for life, and their general policy is not to remarry divorcees in a church ceremony. Some vicars, however, will allow the remarriage of divorced people in their church. An increasing number of vicars are offering a blessing after the remarriage of divorced people in a civil ceremony.

Many **Free Churches** accept divorce and allow remarriage in a church ceremony. These denominations believe that it is not the physical death of one of the partners which ends the marriage. Rather, the marriage ends with the death of the love between the couple. These denominations believe that it is better for the couple to begin their new relationship with the blessing of the church.

What is ...?

An **annulment** in the Roman Catholic Church is the declaration that the marriage never took place properly. It is not a divorce, but a cancellation of the marriage.

Questions

1 Describe and explain the current divorce laws in England and Wales.
2 There has been a rapid increase in divorce in Britain since 1971. Why do you think there has been this increase?
3 Outline, and suggest reasons for, the major differences amongst Christians in their attitude to the remarriage of divorced people.
4 Explain why some Christians might object to divorced people being married in church.
5 A divorce is hard on any children involved. What problems does a divorce cause the children?
6 Why might a Christian feel that they should try to help couples overcome marital difficulties?

The Christian marriage ceremony states that one of the reasons for marriage is that the couple 'may have children and be blessed in caring for them'. When couples marry, they are beginning a new family unit. If they have children, they are ensuring that the human race continues. In Genesis, God instructed that the human race was to 'be fruitful and increase'.

Human babies need to be fed and protected for many years before they can fend for themselves. The family is one way of providing the necessary protection for a baby. Another function of the family is to meet the human needs of love and companionship. Within the family, a child learns how to behave in the society into which they are born. The child will learn the language, the customs and the moral behaviour of that society.

The family has other purposes besides the bringing up of children. The main functions of the family may be summarized as:

'... and bringing them up in accordance with God's will'

- to provide an accepted unit in which reproduction may take place, and in which the children may be reared;

- to provide an economic unit in which everyone is supported, including the children, the sick and the old; and

- to provide emotional support and comfort for the members of that family in times of pleasure and trouble.

The **nuclear** family is usually one or two adults living with their own or adopted children. The **extended** family includes grandparents, aunts and uncles, as well as nephews and nieces and cousins. In many societies the extended family lives together and takes the shared responsibility of bringing up the children, caring for the sick and old members of the family and sharing expenses. There is always someone to turn to when things go wrong, as well as when the family needs to celebrate.

What do you think?

How do you think Christian parents bring up their children 'in accordance with God's will'?

How might the upbringing of a child in a Christian family be different from that of a child in a family with no strong religious beliefs?

 **Activity**

Not all societies are based on a nuclear or extended family. Some people choose to live together because of their shared religious beliefs.

1 Find out more about the Christian community of Taizé.
2 In groups, imagine that you are taking part in the BBC programme *Songs of Praise*, which is to be broadcast from Taizé. You will need the interviewer, one of the community of monks, a Christian teenager and a non-Christian teenager staying with the community. The interviewer will try to find out during the programme why each person has chosen to stay with the community, and what life in the community involves for him or her.

Sometimes the family breaks down and children are left with no one to care for them. A hundred years ago, children with no one to care for them would end up living on the streets. A Christian called Dr Thomas Barnardo decided that God wanted him to work with destitute children. His work developed into the organization now called Barnardo's.

Barnardo's puts into practice the Christian teaching of helping those in need. It seeks to show 'love for my neighbour' by keeping families together. The aim of the organization is:

> to provide and develop in consultation with statutory and other agencies, and in partnership with parents, selected services for children and young people in need and their families on a regional basis. These services, by their nature and by evaluation of their effectiveness, should endeavour to extend knowledge and improve practice.

Dr Thomas Barnardo, who founded the organization named after him which still helps children

 What do you think?

1 Explain, in your own words, the aims of Barnardo's.
2 Explain why you think that Christians are involved with the work of Barnardo's. Support your answer with biblical teaching.

 Questions

1 What are the main functions of the family?
2 a What is a nuclear family?
  b What is an extended family?
3 What differences will there be between a trained nurse caring for an elderly man and a loving daughter caring for her aged father? Give reasons for your answer.
4 Why do you think Christians feel they must help families to overcome their problems? Support your answer with examples of problems which Christians might help families to overcome.

 Activity

Imagine that you are a journalist for your local paper. Research the work of Barnardo's in your area. Write an article for your paper about the organization's current projects.

6: Love Takes Many Forms

When parents grow old

The fifth commandment states, 'Honour thy father and thy mother.' This commandment contains two instructions from God. Children are to obey and respect their parents when they are young. When they grow up, children are to respect and care for their elderly parents.

'Honour thy father and thy mother'

If people live together as an extended family it is very easy to care for the elderly members of the family. There will be several younger people around to keep the older people company. It means that the family can share the nursing of the elderly. In China, three generations of a family may live together and the oldest member of the family is given the greatest respect.

In Britain, as well as in other Western countries, members of families are often scattered throughout the country. Old people often end up living in special homes, cared for by nurses or care assistants. This is an example of **ageism**.

 What is ...?

Ageism is to treat people differently because of their age.

What do you think?

Why do you think it has become acceptable in Britain for old people to live in special homes, rather than with their families?

Do you think that some Christians believe it is wrong to put an aged parent in a home? Give reasons for your opinion.

Many retired people have to live on a small pension. This means that they cannot afford to buy enough food or to keep themselves warm in winter. Many old people are lonely because they have no family near by, and many of their friends have died. The mobility of some old people may be restricted, and they become housebound.

People are living longer, and the number of old and frail people is increasing each year. These people will have to rely on others to try to improve the quality of their life.

 **Activity**

List all the ways in which people are treated differently because of their age. You may include both young, middle-aged and old people in your list.

 What do you think?

Do you think that it is the portrayal in advertisements and television programmes that 'young is beautiful' which has led to ageism, or are there other reasons?

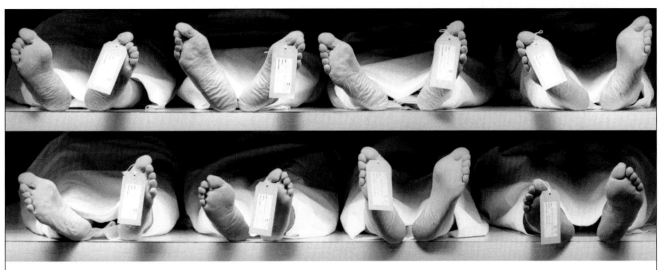

THOUSANDS OF ELDERLY PEOPLE WILL STOP FEELING THE COLD THIS WINTER

Don't let the winter kill. Call 0800 75 00 75

Help the Aged

'Feeling sorry's not enough'

Activity

The parable of the sheep and the goats teaches that Christians will be judged on how they have helped those in need. Christians believe that this includes caring for the elderly.

Make a list of the ways in which people could help the elderly.

Help the Aged is an organization which helps the elderly. Help the Aged raises money to provide the extra care needed by elderly people. The organization seeks to provide suitable homes for aged people, clinics and day centres. Mini-buses are purchased to provide transport for old people. Another aim of the organization is to campaign to improve the life of the elderly by persuading the government to improve their welfare and pensions.

Activity

In groups, organize an activity to raise money for Help the Aged. The group will need to:

- publicize why they are raising the money;
- organize how the money will be raised;
- find out the address of the local branch of Help the Aged to which the money raised can be sent.

Questions

1 What is ageism?
2 List **three** ways in which society discriminates against the elderly.
3 Why do Christians feel that they must help the aged? Support your answer with biblical teaching.
4 What could old people contribute to society? Support your answer with examples.

Do you understand...

what Christians mean by love?

Task 1

On one occasion Jesus said, 'Love your neighbour.' On another occasion he said, 'The greatest love a person can have for his friends is to give his life for them.' At the Last Supper he commanded his apostles to 'love one another'. In the Sermon on the Mount, Jesus warned against 'lustful thoughts'. In each case Jesus is referring to a different type of love.

1 Refer back to page 66 and explain the different Greek words for love.
2 In the quotations above, Jesus refers to two of the Greek words for love. Which two kinds of love does Jesus think people should have for each other?
3 In what ways do you think Jesus put his teaching of 'love your neighbour' into practice? Give specific examples in your answer.

Task 2

Below is a typical letter written in a magazine to an agony aunt. Read the letter and then answer the questions that follow.

Dear Claire,

I am sixteen years old and have been going out with David for three months. We have got on very well until recently, but now he wants me to have sex with him. David says that I cannot love him if I don't want sleep with him. I do love him very much and I am afraid of losing him. I am still a virgin and want to wait until I am married before I have sexual intercourse. I do not know what to do.

Please help me.

Yours

A worried teenager

1 What reply do you think that the agony aunt should give to the teenage girl?
2 Do you think the answer a Christian would give to the teenager would be different from that which would be given by a person with no religious beliefs? Give reasons for your answer.

3 There is a growing movement in the USA to remain a virgin until marriage. Why do you think that many Christian teenagers have joined this movement?

4 Why do some Christians still believe that sex outside marriage is wrong? What are some of the biblical teachings that could be used in an argument supporting this position?

Task 3

1 What vows do couples take in a Christian marriage ceremony?
2 Explain the meaning of these vows.
3 Do you think that taking vows before God will make people try harder to make their marriage work? Give reasons for your opinion.

Task 4

1 Why do marriages break up?
2 What can the Christian church do to reduce the number of divorces in Britain?
3 'Marriage is an outdated institution.' Discuss this statement.

Task 5

During a child's baptism, the parents and godparents make promises on the child's behalf. They agree to 'renounce evil', to 'repent sin' and to 'turn to Christ'. They agree to bring the child up as a Christian.

1 How would you expect the parents and godparents to bring up the child as a Christian?
2 How would you expect the life of a child in a Christian family to be different from a child whose parents do not follow any religious practices? Include in your answer specific examples of the differences you think there will be.
3 Do you think a couple whose marriage is not working should stay together for the sake of the children? Give reasons for your answer, showing that you have thought about more than one point of view.

Task 6

Dr Barnardo had a vocation to provide homes for destitute children.

1 What is a vocation?
2 Why do you think Dr Barnardo's Christian beliefs led him to help homeless children?

Task 7

1 What role do you think grandparents can play in a family?
2 Why do you think that it is easier to raise money for children's charities than it is for charities that help the elderly?
3 Why do you think that more elderly people than young people attend Christian churches?

Topic 1

What is prejudice and discrimination?

What is ...?

Prejudice is a pre-judgement, a feeling and attitude people have towards an individual, a group or a race of people, before they know much about them. It is a biased opinion against someone or something for no logical reason.

Stereotyping is a fixed mental image about a group. Stereotyping is the belief that all members of a group conform to the same pattern.

Activity

1 Look at the people in the picture. For each person decide:
   a their occupation;
   b their social class;
   c their favourite television programme;
   d how they vote.
2 Compare your answers with the rest of the class.

You may have judged the people in the picture by their appearance. This is **stereotyping**.

What do you think?

Do you think your judgement of the people in the picture would have been different if you knew that they were students taking part in Rag Week activities?

The opinions we hold may be based on ideas we have learnt from our parents, from people at school or from the mass media. **Prejudicial** opinions may be based on evidence from personal experience, or the acceptance of other people's prejudices. Prejudicial opinions may be based on one incident alone. For example, a person robbed on holiday in a foreign country may come to the decision that all people in that country are thieves.

What do you think?

How prejudiced are you? Find out by listing your prejudices. You must be honest with yourself.

Discrimination is an action taken against an individual or a group of people as the result of prejudice. Discrimination means that the group is treated differently because of the prejudice.

Discrimination occurs if one group is treated differently because of prejudice. Discrimination includes not giving people equal opportunities in education, housing, employment or political representation. People experience prejudice and discrimination on the grounds of colour, race, gender, age and disability.

People who experience prejudice suffer distress and suffering. Prejudice results in the destruction of property, violence and even murder. The Nazi regime made a decision to rid the world of 'Jewish blood'. It is estimated that six million Jews were killed as part of this policy. Many of the Jews died in the gas chambers of concentration camps like Belsen and Auschwitz. The Jews call this event the **Holocaust.**

Steven Spielberg made a film called *Schindler's List*. It is the true story of Oskar Schindler, who was a member of the Nazi party. Oskar wanted to get rich by using cheap Jewish labour in his factory. When he saw what was happening to the Jews he felt that he had to do something to save them. He managed to save 1,100 Jews during the Holocaust by using the profits he had made at the beginning of the war. By the end of the war he was penniless but he is remembered in Israel as a hero.

Liam Neeson as Oskar Schindler in the film *Schindler's List*

What do you think?

Maria Peleg-Marianska was a Jewess who worked in secret to help fellow Jews in Poland. She was surprised that people who were not Jews were willing to risk their lives to help them. She said, 'One is challenged to think whether in similar circumstances one would have found the inner resources to act as they did.'

Maria worked to help people of her race. In the quotation, she is wondering why non-Jews helped her people. She wonders if she would have risked her life for people of another race. Why do you think many Gentiles (non-Jews) risked their lives to help Jews?

Questions

1 Define prejudice, discrimination and stereotyping.
2 Explain the difference between prejudice and discrimination, and give examples.
3 Why can laws stop discrimination but not prejudice?
4 Why do people become prejudiced?
5 What was the Holocaust?
6 Many Christians have worked to end prejudice. What reasons do you think they would give for their involvement in such campaigns?

Topic 2

Racial prejudice

What is...?

Racial prejudice is pre-judgement about a particular race – the belief that one group of people is inferior based solely on their colour or race.

Scientifically there is no difference between races. Despite scientific research investigating and charting blood groups, bone structure and brain sizes, scientists have found no biological characteristics that belong exclusively to any one group of the world's people. In the past, there have been attempts to define races to show one group as inferior. The treatment of the Jews by the Nazi Party is one example.

Some Christians look to the story of Adam and Eve as evidence that all races descend from the same ancestors. God did not create different races of people at the time of creation, but one man and one woman. The story is teaching that in God's eyes human beings belong to one family. Other Christians would argue that God created through a process of evolution and that mankind is part of the whole animal world. In both cases, Christians believe that if one race is treated as inferior, then this prejudice goes against God's plan, and is a sin.

What is...?

The **Old Commonwealth** refers to those countries that gained their independence from Britain before the First World War, such as Australia, Canada and New Zealand.

The **New Commonwealth** refers to those countries have gained their independence from Britain since the Second World War, such as India and Pakistan.

All races are alike

Activity

1 In groups, make a list of the causes of racial prejudice.
2 Report your group's list back to the rest of the class.
3 Write down the class list.

Britain has frequently accepted immigrants from different races. Before the Second World War the majority of immigrants came from the **Old Commonwealth**. Between 1951 and 1961 the majority of immigrants came from the **New Commonwealth**.

There have been various suggestions as to how to treat immigrants. Four of the models suggested include:

Exclusivism, which seeks to achieve racial purity in a nation by sending all immigrants back to their homelands. There are white racist groups in Britain which support this model.

Complete assimilation is the opposite model to exclusivism. The aim of this model is to absorb immigrants into the community so that the immigrant race loses its identity and adopts the culture of the country.

Segregation allows immigration but keeps the races apart. Each racial group is able to keep their culture but never gets to know the other race.

Integration allows the immigrant group to keep its cultural identity. All the races live side by side with equal opportunities.

 What do you think?

> Which of the models suggesting ways to treat immigrants do you think most Christians would support? Give reasons for your choice, supported by biblical and Christian teaching.

In Britain, the aim is integration. Several acts have been passed to stop discrimination on the grounds of race.

The Race Relations Act 1976 makes it illegal to discriminate on the grounds of colour, race or nationality. It is illegal to discriminate in the fields of employment, housing, education and the provision of goods, facilities and services. The Commission for Racial Equality was set up under the Race Relations Act, to deal with complaints of discrimination.

The Act distinguishes between direct and indirect discrimination. Direct discrimination is to treat one race differently to another. Keeping a job open only to one race would be direct discrimination. Indirect discrimination is an action that puts one racial group at a disadvantage. An employer who only promotes those with a good command of English when it is not required for the position is guilty of indirect discrimination.

 What do you think?

> Do you think the Race Relations Act 1976 has stopped prejudice and discrimination in Britain? Give reasons for your answer, showing that you have thought about more than one point of view.

 Questions

> 1 What is racial prejudice?
> 2 What are the differences between the Old and New Commonwealths?
> 3 List **three** problems which some immigrants from the New Commonwealth meet in Britain.
> 4 The Race Relations Act 1976 tries to stop discrimination in Britain.
>   **a** Summarize the key aspects of the act.
>   **b** How successful do you think this act has been in limiting racial discrimination in Britain?
> 5 List **three** examples of racial discrimination, which are against the law in Britain today.
> 6 What could an individual Christian do to stop racial discrimination?

Topic 3 — Christian teaching about prejudice

Activity

Find out the relationship which existed between the majority of Jews and the Romans at the time of Jesus.

Jesus taught that racial prejudice is against God's wishes. It is a sin. The incident of the healing of the Roman centurion's servant (below) teaches that it is possible for people of different races and religions to live together in harmony, respecting each other's beliefs.

The Romans worshipped many gods, but the Jews only believed in the one God. Jews did not enter the homes of Gentiles for fear of being made 'unclean' in a spiritual sense. This attitude might have offended some people, but the centurion understood that it was part of their beliefs.

The Incident of the Centurion's Servant (Luke 7:1–10)

When Jesus had finished saying all this in the hearing of the people, he entered Capernaum. There a centurion's servant, whom his master valued highly, was sick and about to die. The centurion heard of Jesus and sent some elders of the Jews to him, asking him to come and heal his servant. When they came to Jesus, they pleaded earnestly with him, "This man deserves to have you do this, because he loves our nation and has built our synagogue." So Jesus went with them.

He was not far from the house when the centurion sent friends to say to him: "Lord, don't trouble yourself, for I do not deserve to have you come under my roof. That is why I did not even consider myself worthy to come to you. But say the word, and my servant will be healed. For I myself am a man under authority, with soldiers under me. I tell this one, 'Go,' and he goes; and that one, 'Come,' and he comes. I say to my servant, 'Do this,' and he does it."

When Jesus heard this, he was amazed at him, and turning to the crowd following him, he said, "I tell you, I have not found such great faith even in Israel." Then the men who had been sent returned to the house and found the servant well.

Questions

1 Why did the Jews want to help the Roman centurion?
2 How did the Roman centurion show respect for Judaism (the Jewish faith)?
3 Why did Jesus say that the Roman centurion had more faith than anyone else?
4 How could you connect this incident to race relations in Britain today?

 *Activity*

> Before you read the parable of the good Samaritan, find out why Samaritans and Jews were enemies. It will help you to understand why Jesus chose a Samaritan as the 'hero' of the story.

The Golden Rule taught that you treat others as you would want them to treat you. In the story of the good Samaritan, Jesus used a Samaritan to teach that 'my neighbour' is everyone. Jesus had two supposed good men ignoring the needs of the injured man. The help comes from the man's supposed enemy.

The Parable of the Good Samaritan (Luke 10:25–37)

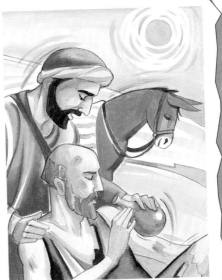

On one occasion an expert in the law stood up to test Jesus. "Teacher," he asked, "what must I do to inherit eternal life?"

"What is written in the Law?" he replied. "How do you read it?"

He answered: "'Love the Lord your God with all your heart and with all your soul and with all your strength and with all your mind'; and, 'Love your neighbour as yourself.'"

"You have answered correctly," Jesus replied. "Do this and you will live."

But he wanted to justify himself, so he asked Jesus, "And who is my neighbour?"

In reply Jesus said: "A man was going down from Jerusalem to Jericho, when he fell into the hands of robbers. They stripped him of his clothes, beat him and went away, leaving him half dead. A priest happened to be going down the same road, and when he saw the man, he passed by on the other side. So too, a Levite, when he came to the place and saw him, passed by on the other side. But a Samaritan, as he travelled, came where the man was; and when he saw him, he took pity on him. He went to him and bandaged his wounds, pouring on oil and wine. Then he put the man on his own donkey, took him to an inn and took care of him. The next day he took out two silver coins and gave them to the innkeeper. 'Look after him,' he said, 'and when I return, I will reimburse you for any extra expense you may have.'

"Which of these three do you think was a neighbour to the man who fell into the hands of robbers?"

The expert in the law answered, "The one who had mercy on him."

Jesus told him, "Go and do likewise."

 *Questions*

1 The lawyer stated the Golden Rule as the way to inherit eternal life. What is the Golden Rule?
2 Why did Jesus choose a Samaritan as the person who helped the injured man?
3 'Which of these three do you think was a neighbour to the man who fell into the hands of robbers?' Answer the question, giving reasons for your answer, showing that you have thought about more than one point of view.
4 What does this parable teach Christians about the treatment of other races?

The Church is for all

The early followers of Jesus believed that Christianity was only for Jews, and therefore any Gentile who wanted to become a Christian had to convert to Judaism first. This meant following the Jewish food laws. The vision of St Peter (see below) changed this attitude.

The man Peter baptized into the Christian faith in Caesarea was called Cornelius. Cornelius was a Roman, who did not follow the Jewish customs. He ate pork and other foods, which the Jews believed were forbidden by God. When he became a Christian Peter did not expect him to follow the Jewish food laws. This was because Peter believed he had been shown in a dream that the Jewish food laws did not apply to Christians.

The Vision of St Peter (Acts 11:1–18)

The apostles and the brothers throughout Judea heard that the Gentiles also had received the word of God. So when Peter went up to Jerusalem, the circumcised believers criticized him and said, "You went into the house of uncircumcised men and ate with them."

Peter began and explained everything to them precisely as it had happened: "I was in the city of Joppa praying, and in a trance I saw a vision. I saw something like a large sheet being let down from heaven by its four corners, and it came down to where I was. I looked into it and saw four-footed animals of the earth, wild beasts, reptiles, and birds of the air. Then I heard a voice telling me, 'Get up, Peter. Kill and eat.'

"I replied, 'Surely not, Lord! Nothing impure or unclean has ever entered my mouth.'

"The voice spoke from heaven a second time, 'Do not call anything impure that God has made clean.' This happened three times, and then it was all pulled up to heaven again.

"Right then three men who had been sent to me from Caesarea stopped at the house where I was staying. The Spirit told me to have no hesitation about going with them. These six brothers also went with me, and we entered the man's house. He told us how he had seen an angel appear in his house and say, 'Send to Joppa for Simon who is called Peter. He will bring you a message through which you and all your household will be saved.'

"As I began to speak, the Holy Spirit came on them as he had come on us at the beginning. Then I remembered what the Lord had said: 'John baptized with water, but you will be baptized with the Holy Spirit.' So if God gave them the same gift as he gave us, who believed in the Lord Jesus Christ, who was I to think that I could oppose God?"

When they heard this, they had no further objections and praised God, saying, "So then, God has granted even the Gentiles repentance unto life."

Peter was criticized by the Church leaders in Jerusalem for eating with Gentiles and for allowing them to become Christian. Peter explained that he had received a vision from God. The vision had made him realize that to be baptized as a Christian did not require conversion to Judaism as well. In his vision Peter heard God saying that Christians need not keep the Jewish traditions and food laws. Peter realized that Gentiles were to be admitted to the Christian Church as well as Jews.

Peter had been shown that the Christian message is for all nations. Christians do not have to change their culture and heritage when they accept the Christian faith, only their behaviour to meet the standards set by Jesus.

? Questions

1. Who was Peter?
2. Cornelius was the first Gentile to be baptized into the Christian faith. What does the word 'Gentile' mean?
3. Why was Peter criticized by the leaders in Jerusalem?
4. What did Peter tell the leaders to stop their criticism?
5. Explain how this incident showed that the Church was no longer regarded as only for one racial group.

Topic 4 Gender issues

 What is...?

Sexism is treating the members of one sex differently because of their sex.

Gender is the sex of something. Gender is to state whether something is male or female.

Sexism is a form of prejudice. Women have felt that they have suffered prejudice and discrimination because of their **gender** for centuries. At the beginning of the 20th century, it was believed that a woman's place was in the home, looking after her husband and children. The majority of girls left school at twelve years of age, and were married by the time that they were twenty-five. There were few job opportunities for women. The majority of women worked in domestic service, shops or textile mills. If men and women did the same work, then women were paid less than men. Women were not given the same opportunities for promotion, as it was believed that they could not perform tasks as efficiently as men or that they would leave to raise a family.

 Activity

1 In groups, make a list of some of the possible causes of prejudice against women.
2 Are there any ways in which men are seen as inferior to women?
3 Report your list back to the rest of the class.

What do you think?

Do you think the feminist movement approves of the Miss World competition? Give reasons for your opinion.

Do you think that men approve of acts such as the Chippendales?

Diana Hayden, Miss World 1997

In the 1960s, the feminist movement began to challenge the stereotyped image of women. The growing pressure from feminists to break down the discrimination of women resulted in two important acts in Britain, which aim to give women equal rights with men.

- The Equal Pay Act 1975 stated that women were to be paid on an equal basis with men who do the same or broadly similar jobs.
- The Sex Discrimination Act 1975 made it illegal to suggest in an advertisement for a job that it was only for men, or only for women. Women and men must be given equal opportunities for promotion within the work place.

At the end of the 20th century, all girls in Britain have the right of education up to sixteen years of age. It is illegal to not give equal opportunities to men and women. The majority of women return to work after the birth of a child, and under the law are to be treated equally to men. There has been a gradual closing of the wage gap between men and women since 1975. There is still a noticeable gap, however, and women are not achieving promotion in equal numbers to men.

Often discrimination has been suggested as a major reason for these differences in earnings and promotion. Others have suggested that women choose certain occupations so that they can balance work and family obligations.

What do you think?

Why do you think there is still a gap between the earnings of men and women?

The pop group the Spice Girls tried to break down the gender barriers. The all-girl band suggest that teenagers should follow their 'girl power' philosophy. The Spice Girls want to show that girls are as good as boys.

Does 'girl power' work?

What do you think?

The Spice Girls have stated that their aim is to bring feminism up to date for the 1990s. Their mission was to show girls could do things as well as boys, if not better.

Do you think that the Spice Girls have achieved their aim? Give reasons for your answer, showing that you have thought about more than one point of view.

The Roman Catholic and Eastern Orthodox Churches do not **ordain** women priests. These Churches believe that only men are suitable to bless and administer the sacrament of Holy Communion. The Church of England has accepted the ordination of women priests, but at the loss of many male priests. Many Protestant churches, including the Methodists and Baptists, allow women to become ministers.

What is ...?

Ordination is the service that makes an individual a leader in the Christian Church.

Questions

1 List **three** forms of discrimination that women might experience in Britain today.
2 Outline the laws in Britain which seek to stop discrimination against women.
3 Do you think that opposition to the ordination of women in some Christian churches is a form of discrimination against women? Give reasons for your answer, showing that you have thought about more than one point of view.

Topic 5

Jesus' attitude to women

Jesus was born into a society where women had a second-class role. Their husbands owned them. Jewish men thanked God daily in their prayers that they had not been born a woman. In a public place a man would not acknowledge a woman, even his wife or daughter. Women were not allowed to worship God alongside men in the synagogue or temple in Jerusalem. Women had a separate area in which to worship.

Jesus' treatment of women contrasted with the accepted attitudes of the time. There are several incidents in the Gospels in which Jesus showed that he believed women were equal to men. It was women who discovered that Jesus had risen from the dead, and one of first people to see Jesus after the Resurrection was Mary Magdalene. Luke's Gospel mentions that Jesus was accompanied on his travels by women, as well as the twelve disciples. In his ministry, Jesus talked to and healed women as naturally as he did men.

The Incident of Mary and Martha (Luke 10:38–42)

As Jesus and his disciples were on their way, he came to a village where a woman named Martha opened her home to him. She had a sister called Mary, who sat at the Lord's feet listening to what he said. But Martha was distracted by all the preparations that had to be made. She came to him and asked, "Lord, don't you care that my sister has left me to do the work by myself? Tell her to help me!"

"Martha, Martha," the Lord answered, "you are worried and upset about many things, but only one thing is needed. Mary has chosen what is better, and it will not be taken away from her."

Women did not sit with men for meals. The women would wait on the men and then eat in the kitchen. A rabbi would not teach women. In this incident, Jesus breaks this rule. He allows Mary to listen to his teaching.

? Questions

1 In the incident of Mary and Martha, which sister behaves in the accepted way, and which sister appears to break the rules?
2 What do you think that Jesus meant when he said, 'Mary has chosen what is better, and it will not be taken away from her'?
3 Why is the incident of Mary and Martha sometimes chosen to support the ordination of women?

The Incident of the Anointing of Jesus (Mark 14:3–9)

While he was in Bethany, reclining at the table in the home of a man known as Simon the Leper, a woman came with an alabaster jar of very expensive perfume, made of pure nard. She broke the jar and poured the perfume on his head.

Some of those present were saying indignantly to one another, "Why this waste of perfume? It could have been sold for more than a year's wages and the money given to the poor." And they rebuked her harshly.

"Leave her alone," said Jesus. "Why are you bothering her? She has done a beautiful thing to me. The poor you will always have with you, and you can help them any time you want. But you will not always have me. She did what she could. She poured perfume on my body beforehand to prepare for my burial. I tell you the truth, wherever the gospel is preached throughout the world, what she has done will also be told, in memory of her."

Jesus allowed a woman to touch him, when she anointed him with expensive oil. This was against usual practice. The event took place three days before Jesus' crucifixion. Many people have seen this anointing as a preparation of his body for burial. The disciples grumbled at the waste of money but Jesus praised her action.

Jesus showed by his reply that he gave credit where it was due, regardless of the person's sex. He showed that both men and women are capable of understanding his teaching. By his actions, Jesus showed that his message is for both men and women.

Questions

1 In your own words, outline the incident of the anointing of Jesus.
2 Why did Jesus say that the woman's action will be 'preached throughout the world'?
3 What do you think this incident teaches about the role of women in Christianity?

Topic 6

Equal opportunities for the disabled

Activity

Look back at the incident of the anointing of Jesus (page 93) and remind yourself what happened.

Jesus was anointed in the home of Simon the Leper. Lepers had to live outside their village or town. They were not allowed to mix with healthy people and had to call out 'unclean, unclean' to warn people not to come near to them.

At the time of Jesus, many skin diseases were classed as **leprosy,** and the unfortunate sufferer had to move out of his or her home. As many of the skin conditions were not leprosy, they disappeared in time. An individual could return home if declared free of the disease by a priest. That Simon is home again means that he was free of the disease. He is still called Simon the Leper and therefore his **disability** has not been forgotten. By visiting his home, Jesus is showing that he regards disabled people as important as the able-bodied.

Activity

List the reasons why people with a disability may sometimes experience prejudice and discrimination.

What is ...?

Leprosy is a mildly infectious disease. It affects the nerves, skin, eyes and nose. If it is untreated, the nerve endings lose feeling, which can lead to deformity.

Disability is the lack of some bodily function. It could be a physical disability such as blindness or a mental disability.

In July 1998 the government unveiled plans for a Disability Rights Commission to ensure civil rights for disabled people. It is felt that disabled people have not the same means to claim equal rights as those who experience prejudice on the grounds of race or gender.

Christians work with many organizations to improve conditions for the disabled. The Shaftesbury Society is an example of one such organization. It provides residential care or support in people's homes. The Shaftesbury Society believes that it is putting Christian teaching into practice by supporting over 2,000 people with a disability in the country.

Activity

1 Find out more about the work of the Shaftesbury Society or another organization that seeks to improve the life of the disabled.
2 Using the information you have discovered, make a five-minute appeal on behalf of the Society. Imagine that it is to be broadcast as the Radio 4 Appeal at 7.55 am one Sunday morning.

The opportunities for disabled people have improved in recent years. The aim is to allow people with handicaps to lead as normal a life as possible. The aim of most charities is to give disabled people as much independence as possible. One of the main problems that disabled people have is access to public buildings.

 ## What do you think?

Do you think that children with physical or mental disabilities should be allowed to attend school alongside children without disabilities? Give reasons for your answer, showing that you have thought about more than one point of view.

Do you think most Christians would agree or disagree with your view? Support your answer with biblical teaching.

 ## Activity

In pairs, find out how difficult it would be for a disabled person to move around your school. Imagine your route around the school (e.g. from your classroom to the dining hall, library or sports hall). What dangers or difficulties would arise for a blind person moving around in your school building?

The parable of the sheep and the goats teaches Christians to care for the needy

 ## Questions

1 Many elderly people are disabled. What are the main problems caused by disability that face the elderly?
2 Why might a Christian consider that they have a duty to care for the elderly? Give examples in your answer.
3 Suggest **three** ways in which a local church could show care for the disabled, and in each case explain why you think it would be an effective way.

Do you understand...

the Christian attitude to prejudice and discrimination?

Task 1

'I knew the people who worked for me. When you know people you have to behave towards them like human beings.' (Oskar Schindler)

1 What reason did Oskar Schindler give for helping the Jews escape the gas chambers?
2 Explain why most Christians would believe that Schindler's action was right. Support your answer with teachings from the Bible.

Task 2

1 **a** Why might some people object to this picture (left) on the grounds of racial prejudice?
  b Why might other people have no difficulty with this picture?
2 Why might some people object to this picture on the grounds of the stereotyping of women?
3 Outline an incident from the life of Jesus, which showed he believed in the equality of women with men.

Task 3

A **Engineering apprenticeships** available at Smithson UK. Boys aged 16 with GCSEs phone 0237 563420 for details.

B Bar staff required at
Doug's Wine Bar.
Applicants must be white.
Phone 785609.

C ## Cleaners wanted
to work in local offices. Men paid £5 per hour and women £3.50.

Apply in writing to CleanEasy, 10 Mean Street, London W1 6YY.

D Serving staff required in school kitchen.
Phone 765401.

1 a Which advertisement breaks the Sex Discrimination Act?
   b How does this advertisement break the law?
2 a Which advertisement breaks the Race Relations Act?
   b How does this advertisement break the law?
3 a Which advertisement breaks the Equal Pay Act?
   b How does this advertisement break the law?
4 a Which advertisement is legal?
   b Rewrite the other advertisements to make them legal and openly
      attractive to everyone.

Task 4

One day Jesus met a Samaritan woman at a well. Look back at pages 87 and
92–3 and remind yourself of the attitude of Jews to Samaritans and women
at the time of Jesus, before reading this extract.

Jesus, tired as he was from the journey, sat down by the well ...

When a Samaritan woman came to draw water, Jesus said to her, "Will you give me a drink?"
(His disciples had gone into the town to buy food.)

The Samaritan woman said to him, "You are a Jew and I am a Samaritan woman. How can you
ask me for a drink?" (For Jews do not associate with Samaritans.)

Jesus answered her, "If you knew the gift of God and who it is that asks you for a drink, you
would have asked him and he would have given you living water."

"Sir," the woman said, "you have nothing to draw with and the well is deep. Where can you get this
living water? Are you greater than our father Jacob, who gave us the well and drank from it himself,
as did also his sons and his flocks and herds?"

Jesus answered, "Everyone who drinks this water will be thirsty again, but whoever drinks the
water I give him will never thirst. Indeed, the water I give him will become in him a spring of
water welling up to eternal life."

The woman said to him, "Sir, give me this water, so that I won't get thirsty and have to keep
coming here to draw water." ...

Jesus declared, "Believe me, woman, a time is coming when you will worship the Father neither on
this mountain nor in Jerusalem. You Samaritans worship what you do not know; we worship what
we do know, for salvation is from the Jews. Yet a time is coming and has now come when the true
worshippers will worship the Father in spirit and truth, for they are the kind of worshippers the
Father seeks. God is spirit, and his worshippers must worship in spirit and in truth."

The woman said, "I know that Messiah" (called Christ) "is coming. When he comes, he will
explain everything to us."

Then Jesus declared, "I who speak to you am he."

Just then his disciples returned and were surprised to find him talking with a woman. But no one
asked, "What do you want?" or "Why are you talking with her?"

(John 4:6–27)

1 Why do you think that the disciples were amazed to find Jesus 'talking
   with a woman'?
2 What do you think that this incident teaches about prejudice and
   discrimination?

Topic 1 Rich and poor countries

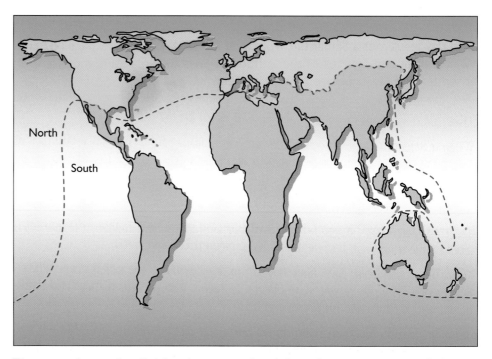

The rich and the poor world

The map shows the division between the rich and poor countries of the world. The rich countries are those countries above the line on the map, and the poor countries are those countries beneath the line. The rich countries are often called the North, or the **developed world**. The poor countries are often called the South, or the **developing world**. Another name used to refer to the developing world is the **Third World**.

The North (the developed world) is made up of countries such as the United Kingdom, the United States of America, Japan and Australia. 25 percent of the world's population live in the rich countries. These countries have 80 percent of the world's wealth. The average life expectancy is 73 years, and the infant death rate is low. There is education for all, access to health care and plenty to eat. The major source of income is industry, and people have a real income 20 percent higher than the people of the South.

The **South** (the developing world) is made up of countries such as Ethiopia, India and Brazil. 75 percent of the world's population live in these countries. These countries have only 20 percent of the world's wealth. The average life expectancy is 50 years old, and the death rate of children under five is high. Few people have the chance of a formal education, and access to health care. At any one time, a quarter of the people are hungry or malnourished. Most people live in poverty and work on the land.

1 Divide a piece of paper into two columns.
2 Label one column The Developed World and the other column The Developing World.
3 Under each heading, list the different features of the rich and the poor countries.
4 Compare the differences between the two columns.

The problems found in the developing countries are hunger, poverty, disease and a population explosion. The richer (developed) countries sometimes act together to help the developing countries. Representatives from all over the world work together to see if the problems of world poverty can be solved.

The belief is that not only do developed countries have a duty to help the poorer developing countries, but also that it is in their interests. If the developing countries become poorer then they will no longer be able to purchase manufactured goods from developed countries. This would reduce the wealth of developed countries. The poorer developing countries need practical help as well as money and goods.

Long-term aid is aid that seeks to overcome the problems of the developing world in such a way that help will not be needed in the future. It includes teaching people how to improve their farming methods and medical care.

Short-term aid is emergency aid. The aid provides supplies such as food and medical aid at the time of a disaster.

Long-term aid is a more permanent solution to the problems of developing countries. The people of the developed world need to be educated about the problems of developing countries and how to solve them. **Short-term aid** has to be provided when a disaster occurs.

1 What other names are used to describe the countries of the North and the South?
2 a Name **two** countries in the North.
  b Name **two** countries in the South.
3 State **three** differences between the countries of the North and the South.
4 State the **four** major problems experienced by people in the South.
5 Why is it in the interests of the rich countries of the North to help the poorer countries of the South?
6 What is the difference between long-term aid and short-term aid?
7 Why would Christians believe that they should help to overcome the problems of the poorer countries?

Topic 2

The problems of the developing world

What do you think?

> To be poor, is not to be able to satisfy basic human needs: food, housing, health, education, job and social participation. The Bible points out that to be poor is the same as to be 'oppressed'.
>
> (World Council of Churches)

What do you think the World Council of Churches means by this statement?

Poverty

The developing world has only one fifth of the world's income to share between three quarters of the world's population. The outcome is poverty. This poverty is caused by the fact that three quarters of the earnings of developing countries is mainly derived from farming. These products bring in little profit as the market prices tend to be low. The majority of farmers in the poor countries cannot produce enough food to feed their families. The developing countries tend to have few commodities to export. Poverty forms a vicious circle that is difficult to break.

The circle of poverty shows that the problems of sickness, the inability to work and malnutrition are linked. To overcome the problems of poverty, many countries apply to the World Bank for financial help. The debts are made worse because the country's debt increases, owing to the interest owed on the debt. The result is that the developing countries owe money to various banks, countries and the International Monetary Fund, which they have no hope of repaying.

Activity

Draw the circle of poverty.

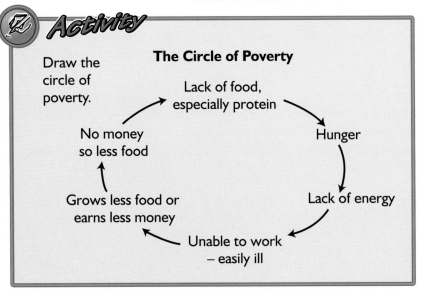

The Circle of Poverty

- Lack of food, especially protein
- Hunger
- Lack of energy
- Unable to work – easily ill
- Grows less food or earns less money
- No money so less food

What do you think?

The Archbishop of Canterbury believes that the banks should write off the debts of developing countries. He believes that this is the only way in which the developing countries will escape the poverty trap. What do you think? Give reasons for your answer, showing that you have thought about more than one point of view.

The cancelling of the debts to the banks may be one way to solve the problems of poverty. The other solution is to break the circle of poverty. Developed countries could help to achieve this by providing a market for goods from the developing countries. At the moment developed countries pay low prices for the raw materials so that the manufacturer is able to make a high profit. For example, for every jar of coffee sold the producing country receives only 37 percent of the selling price and the manufacturer and retailer the rest.

If the developing countries are to get out of the poverty trap, the producers need to sell their goods directly to the retailers. The goods have to be sold in this country at a price that would ensure the workers in the country of origin get a fair wage. Aid agencies such as OXFAM and Christian Aid sell goods in this manner. Commodities sold in this manner are coffee, tea, fruit juice and rice. These agencies encourage trade by selling manufactured goods as well such as basketwork, jewellery and pottery.

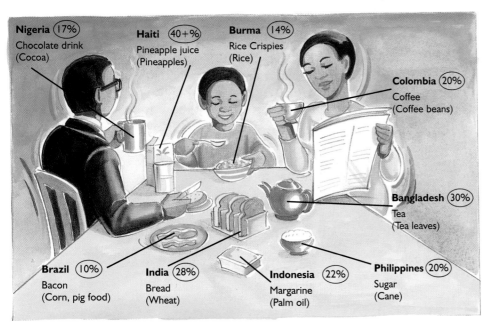

Are you eating at the expense of others? This illustration shows the country of origin of many of our breakfast foods and drinks, and the percentage of the population in that country who are undernourished.

Questions

1 What are the causes of poverty in the developing world?
2 How does the circle of poverty stop people in the developing world from overcoming poverty?
3 How could the World Bank help developing countries to overcome poverty?
4 How could an individual help to overcome poverty in the developing world?
5 Suggest ways in which the Christian Church could help to overcome poverty in the developing world.

Hunger

The world's food problem is both a shortage and a surplus. There is enough food in the world if it is shared out equally. The European Union (EU) keeps a surplus of food to ensure high prices for farmers. If the farmers produce a surplus of a particular food then the surplus is hoarded to keep prices high. In the past these surpluses have included grain and butter. These have been referred to as 'grain mountains' and 'butter mountains'.

The EU may have a surplus of food, but by contrast people in developing countries suffer **starvation** and **malnutrition**. In the developing world, 35,000 people die of hunger each day. Four hundred and fifty million people go to bed hungry each night.

The richer countries and multi-national companies exploit the developing countries. Coffee, sugar, cotton, rubber, fats and oils are crops from developing countries. These crops are sold at low prices to the developed countries. In addition, the governments of developing countries often force farmers to grow crops to sell rather than food for their family to eat. The sale of crops such as rice to developed countries brings in revenue to the country.

The causes of hunger

There are many causes of hunger. These include:

- In many developing countries, there is a lack of water to irrigate crops. For example, this was a cause of **famine** in Ethiopia.
- In other developing countries there may be too much water. Floods occur which wash out the crops. This is a frequent problem in Bangladesh.
- The transportation of food from one area to another may be difficult. This may be because there are poor roads, or the transport may have to pass through war zones.
  - Many developing countries do not make full use of natural resources, such as fish.
  - There is a lack of mechanization because the countries cannot afford machines. Lack of equipment such as tractors means a lower yield from the land.
  - There is little knowledge of ways to increase the yield from an area of land.
  - 'Cash crops' are grown for sale abroad rather than to feed the population.
  - Cultural problems may result in some available foods not being used. For example, the cow is sacred to Hindus.
  - There may be a lack of suitable storage of food in hot climates, so any surplus is lost.
  - There are many diseases and pests in these countries. Diseases and pests destroy crops and kill animals. For example, the tsetse fly causes sleeping sickness.

What is...?

Starvation is having insufficient food to sustain life. The condition often leads to death.

Malnutrition is the result of having inadequate food or the wrong type of food to maintain a healthy diet.

Famine occurs when there is a shortage of food to feed people in a particular area at a specific time. Starvation results and people die.

These statements are nothing more than myths

Aid agencies can send food at the time of a disaster, but this is only a short-term solution. If people in the developing world are to become independent of aid, then they need more permanent solutions to their problems.

Solutions to the problem of hunger

Possible solutions to the problem of hunger in the developing world include:

* Teaching the people new farming methods, such as ways of maintaining good fertilization of the land, selective breeding of cattle, or better seeds so that the land gives a higher yield of food.
* Researching into pest control and eradication of disease in these areas so more plants and animals survive.
* Finding new sources of food. In recent years, the soya bean has been used as an excellent source of protein.
* Improving the transportation and storage of food so that there is more food available throughout the year.

 Activity

Write to an aid agency working in the developing world to find out what type of projects they support.

 What do you think?

'The United Kingdom's top ten supermarkets make more money in a year than the world's 35 poorest countries combined.' (Christian Aid)

If the statement from Christian Aid is true, what do you think that the supermarkets should do? Give reasons for your answer, showing that you have thought about more than one point of view.

 **Activity**

Design a T-shirt which could be worn during a campaign to encourage managers of supermarkets and shoppers to ask for fair wages and working conditions for the people in the developing countries who produce the goods that the supermarkets sell.

Questions

1 What are 'grain' and 'butter' mountains?
2 What evidence would a Christian use to support a belief that these food mountains are wrong?
3 State and explain **four** causes of hunger in the developing world.
4 State and explain **four** ways in which more food could be grown in the developing world.

8: The Developing or Third World

Health

Poverty and the lack of adequate food in the developing world results in poor health. People are more prone to disease and ill health. Children need more protein than adults because they are growing fast. If they do not get it, they can be harmed both physically and mentally. In the poorer countries, the death rate of children under five years is high. Children die because they are malnourished and lack resistance to disease. The children who survive will be affected for life by poor feeding in their early years.

A typical three-year-old in a developing country will have had up to sixteen bouts of diarrhoea, ten infections of the chest and throat, an attack of measles and conjunctivitis and perhaps malaria or meningitis. For each child this is an average of one illness every three months. The death rate of children under four is much higher in the developing countries than it is in Britain. Poor health as the result of poverty continues as the individual gets older. The average life expectancy in these countries is only 50 years, whereas in Britain it is 73 years.

The causes of poor health

There are many other causes of poor health in the developing countries. These include:

A child collecting contaminated drinking water

- Drinking water is in short supply or unfit to drink in the developing world. The problem is greatest in heavily populated areas. Two thousand million people, half the world's population, do not have access to clean and adequate water supply. Even more people lack proper sanitation. 80 percent of all the diseases of the world are water related.
- The people suffer from poor health, but they have less access to medical care than the people of developed countries. There is a shortage of trained doctors and nurses. The lack of adequate medical care causes conditions to become worse, as patients often receive inadequate treatment.
- There are many insects which transmit diseases. For example, the mosquito spreads malaria.
- Few children are immunized against common ailments such as measles, which can kill.

Solutions to the problems of ill health

The possible solutions to the problems of ill health in the developing world include:

- Promoting proper nutrition so that people have better resistance to disease.
- Providing clean water and adequate sanitation so that the water-borne diseases are removed, at the same time as educating people about the need for hygiene in the home.

- Introducing a programme of immunization against the six common diseases of childhood.
- Training people from each village in basic first aid and health care to avoid medical conditions becoming worse.
- Educating the communities about common health problems and how to treat them.
- Training more nurses and doctors, and introducing health workers on the spot to deal with basic treatments.
- Introducing mobile clinics, for example for the antenatal care of pregnant women, to improve the standard of health care.
- Researching into appropriate health techniques for the regions.

A new well in San Pedro

Activity

One problem of providing people in the developing world with information is that few people can read. Design a leaflet that could be circulated in villages to raise their awareness of the link between unclean water and disease. Remember that it needs to be simple and mainly in picture format.

Questions

1 Explain **three** problems that cause poor health in the developing world.
2 Describe how overseas agencies deal with the problem of disease in developing countries.
3 Do you think that Christians should spend vast sums of money on the upkeep of their church buildings when there are so many starving and needy people in developing countries? Give reasons for your answer, showing that you have considered more than one point of view.

The population explosion

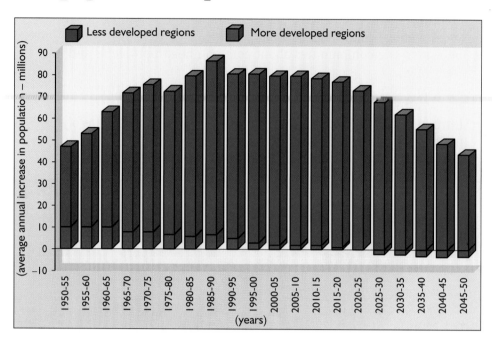

The average annual increase in world population, 1950–2050

What do you think?

Why do you think that the population of the developing world increased significantly between 1985 and 1990?

Over one million people are added to the population of the world every five days. Nearly 98 percent of the annual increase in population occurs in the developing countries. Seventy-four of these countries are on a course that will lead to the doubling of the country's population by the end of the century.

The rapid population growth in the poorest countries of the world means that any progress made in food production or health care is lost. The countries that are least able to overcome the problems of poverty, hunger and disease, are the countries with the most rapid expansion in population.

The causes of the population explosion

There are many causes of the population explosion in the developing world. These include:

- People in the developing world tend to have large families to make sure that there are labourers to tend the land and someone to care for them in old age.
- The governments of these countries want manpower for their armies.
- The religious beliefs of many of these countries do not encourage the use of contraceptives.
- Recent improvements in medical care, nutrition and hygiene have led to many more children surviving infancy.
- The improvement in medical care, nutrition and hygiene has lowered the death rate in these countries so that more people are living longer.

Any progress made by these countries in overcoming poverty is limited as long as the population grows faster than the improvements introduced.

Activity

1 Copy out the graph of the world's population between 1950 and 2050 (above).
2 Colour the population growth in the developing regions.

A World Fertility Survey has provided information on the problems and put forward possible solutions.

Solutions to the population explosion

There are several possible solutions to the population explosion in the developing world. These include:

- Education is one of the major ways in which many problems in the developing world can be overcome. If people understand why it is better to limit the size of their families then the birth rate will fall.
- The education of women reduces the population because educated women tend to have smaller families. Poverty in the developing world means little money to build schools, colleges and universities, to train more teachers and to buy the books and equipment needed by teachers and pupils. The culture of some countries does not regard the education of girls as important. This attitude must be changed if the population of developing countries is to be reduced.
- The attitude to large families needs to be changed. People need to be encouraged to see the advantages of a smaller family. People need to realize that with better health care and nutrition more of their children will survive. In some countries, advertising campaigns are used to show the difference between a small healthy family and a larger unhealthy one.
- The education of people about the use of contraception might help to reduce the population. Contraceptives need to be widely available and in a variety of forms which the people can understand how to use. In India men have been encouraged to have a vasectomy when they have had two children.

Solving the population explosion would make children healthier

 ## What do you think?

Does it matter if the world becomes overcrowded?

 ## Questions

1 State the reasons why the population explosion is a problem for the developing world.
2 Explain why some Christians are against the use of artificial means of birth control in the developing world.
3 Why do you think that other Christians believe that the only way to deal with the population explosion is by compulsory birth control?
4 Explain **four** ways in which the population explosion in the developing world may be overcome.

Topic 3

The Christian response to the problems of the developing world

Jesus taught that Christians should help people in need. This includes the starving people of the world.

The Parable of the Rich Fool (Luke 12:13–21)

Someone in the crowd said to him, "Teacher, tell my brother to divide the inheritance with me."

Jesus replied, "Man, who appointed me a judge or an arbiter between you?" Then he said to them, "Watch out! Be on your guard against all kinds of greed; a man's life does not consist in the abundance of his possessions."

And he told them this parable: "The ground of a certain rich man produced a good crop. He thought to himself, 'What shall I do? I have no place to store my crops.'

"Then he said, 'This is what I'll do. I will tear down my barns and build bigger ones, and there I will store all my grain and my goods. And I'll say to myself, "You have plenty of good things laid up for many years. Take life easy; eat, drink and be merry."'

"But God said to him, 'You fool! This very night your life will be demanded from you. Then who will get what you have prepared for yourself?'

"This is how it will be with anyone who stores up things for himself but is not rich toward God."

This parable is teaching the dangers of the pursuit of wealth. The farmer puts all his efforts into getting rich, and when he thinks he can now retire, and enjoy his wealth, he dies. Someone who has not worked for them inherits all his possessions. He has done nothing that is of value in God's eyes. He has not built up 'treasures in heaven'. Christians will be judged not on the size of their bank balance, but on how they have helped those less fortunate.

Questions

1 Why is the man in the parable referred to as a 'fool'?
2 Why is he 'not rich toward God'?
3 What 'treasures in heaven' should he have built up?
4 What lesson might this parable have for Christians in today's world?

The Parable of the Rich Man and Lazarus (Luke 16:19–31)

There was a rich man who was dressed in purple and fine linen and lived in luxury every day. At his gate was laid a beggar named Lazarus, covered with sores and longing to eat what fell from the rich man's table. Even the dogs came and licked his sores.

The time came when the beggar died and the angels carried him to Abraham's side. The rich man also died and was buried. In hell, where he was in torment, he looked up and saw Abraham far away, with Lazarus by his side. So he called to him, "Father Abraham, have pity on me and send Lazarus to dip the tip of his finger in water and cool my tongue, because I am in agony in this fire."

But Abraham replied, "Son, remember that in your lifetime you received your good things, while Lazarus received bad things, but now he is comforted here and you are in agony. And besides all this, between us and you a great chasm has been fixed, so that those who want to go from here to you cannot, nor can anyone cross over from there to us."

He answered, "Then I beg you, father, send Lazarus to my father's house, for I have five brothers. Let him warn them, so that they will not also come to this place of torment."

Abraham replied, "They have Moses and the Prophets; let them listen to them."

"No, father Abraham," he said, "but if someone from the dead goes to them, they will repent."

He said to him, "If they do not listen to Moses and the Prophets, they will not be convinced even if someone rises from the dead."

The rich man finds himself in hell, not because he was rich but because his wealth blinded him to the needs of others. He was in comfort and failed to notice Lazarus at his gate. The man was told that the scriptures contain warnings of the punishment that awaits those who ignore the needy. If people listen to the prophets then they know that all wealth belongs to God, and must be used as God would wish. People must not be greedy.

Questions

1 Why is the rich man sent to hell when he dies?
2 Why do you think the parable mentions people not listening to a messenger who rises from the dead?
3 How does the teaching of the parable of the rich man and Lazarus apply to the problems of the relations between the world's richest and poorest countries?

Activity

Find out about the way in which the early Church was organized, in the years following the resurrection of Jesus, to make sure that no Christian was in need.

Jesus taught that everyone who has wealth must share with everyone who has nothing. The early Church put this teaching into practice by sharing all that they had, to make sure that no one was in need. The incident of Barnabas (below) is an example of how a convert to Christianity shared his wealth with those in need in the community.

The Incident of Barnabas and the Early Church (Acts 4:32–37)

All the believers were one in heart and mind. No one claimed that any of his possessions was his own, but they shared everything they had. With great power the apostles continued to testify to the resurrection of the Lord Jesus, and much grace was upon them all. There were no needy persons among them. For from time to time those who owned lands or houses sold them, brought the money from the sales and put it at the apostles' feet, and it was distributed to anyone as he had need.

Joseph, a Levite from Cyprus, whom the apostles called Barnabas (which means Son of Encouragement), sold a field he owned and brought the money and put it at the apostles' feet.

Questions

1 What does the action of Barnabas show about the way in which the early Church looked after its members?
2 What did Barnabas do to help the needy in the Church?
3 How does this action apply to the way in which developed countries should help the developing countries?

 What do you think?

Why do some people who win large sums of money on the National Lottery not use some of it to help people in need? Give reasons for your answer, and show that you have thought about more than one point of view.

Do you think being a Christian might make any difference to the way in which a winner used their winnings? Use teachings from the Bible to support your answer.

Christian Aid

Many Christians today believe that they can follow the example of Barnabas by helping to raise money for the work of Christian Aid.

Christian Aid was founded in 1945 by British churches to help the refugees in Europe following the Second World War. Later it extended its work to help those in need throughout the world. Christian Aid does not have projects of its own, but supports the projects of others, regardless of religious belief or nationality. Christian Aid puts Jesus' teaching into practice by treating anyone in need as their 'neighbour'.

Christian Aid raises money by a door-to-door envelope collection during Christian Aid week, as well as by sponsored events, voluntary donations and government grants. Most of the money raised supports projects designed to tackle the poverty in the developing countries of the world.

Most of the projects supported are long-term aid. These projects seek to tackle the root causes of the problems in the developing world. For example, one of the major causes of ill health is unclean water. Christian Aid supports projects to sink wells that provide a clean water supply to villages. Christian Aid prefers to fund local organizations in an area of need, as they believe that this is how best to meet local needs. Using a local labour force also provides work for the area, and therefore is another method of overcoming poverty.

Christian Aid also provides emergency aid at the time of disaster. This includes food and medical supplies.

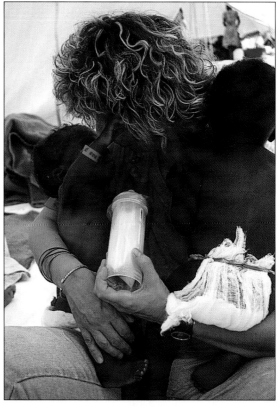

We believe in life before death

1 Find out more about the work of either Christian Aid, Tear Fund or CAFOD.
2 Use the information you have researched to write a detailed account of:
   a how the organization you have chosen might help with emergency aid at the time of a disaster;
   b how the organization you have chosen might help with long-term aid to overcome:
      (i) poverty;
      (ii) famine;
      (iii) health problems; and
      (iv) the population explosion.
3 a Explain ways in which the organization makes people in Britain aware of its work.
   b Explain how the organization raises its funds.

Do you understand...

the Christian response to the developing world?

Task 1

1 Outline the parable of the sheep and the goats (pages 60–61).
2 How does the teaching of this parable relate to the problems of the developing world?

Task 2

The prayer and picture below are published by Christian Aid to focus people's thoughts on the problems of the developing world.

O God, to whom we owe more than we can count, in our desire to control all that will come to be, we hold your other children in the grip of debt which they cannot repay, and make them suffer now the poverty we dread. Do not hold us to our debts, but unchain our fear, that we may release others into an open future of unbounded hope through Jesus Christ our Saviour.

Amen

(Janet Morley)

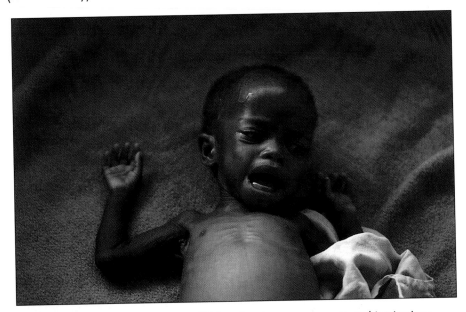

Each baby in Tanzania already owes £120 to foreign governments and institutions

1 Explain the problem in the developing world to which this picture and prayer are referring.
2 What does the caption mean when it states the baby 'owes £120 to foreign governments and institutions'?
3 What does the prayer mean when it states that we owe God more than we can count?
4 Why does this prayer teach that Christians must overcome debt?
5 Do you think that the 'other children' should be released from the 'grip of debt'? Give reasons for your answer, showing that you have thought about more than one point of view.

Task 3

Read the following account of the Feeding of the Five Thousand, and answer the questions which follow.

When Jesus landed and saw a large crowd, he had compassion on them, because they were like sheep without a shepherd. So he began teaching them many things.

By this time it was late in the day, so his disciples came to him. "This is a remote place," they said, "and it's already very late. Send the people away so they can go to the surrounding countryside and villages and buy themselves something to eat."

But he answered, "You give them something to eat."

They said to him, "That would take eight months of a man's wages! Are we to go and spend that much on bread and give it to them to eat?"

"How many loaves do you have?" he asked. "Go and see."

When they found out, they said, "Five – and two fish."

Then Jesus directed them to have all the people sit down in groups on the green grass. So they sat down in groups of hundreds and fifties. Taking the five loaves and the two fish and looking up to heaven, he gave thanks and broke the loaves. Then he gave them to his disciples to set before the people. He also divided the two fish among them all. They all ate and were satisfied, and the disciples picked up twelve basketfuls of broken pieces of bread and fish. The number of the men who had eaten was five thousand.

(Mark 6:34–44)

1 Describe the incident of the Feeding of the Five Thousand in your own words.
2 Many Christians describe the Feeding of the Five Thousand as a miracle.
    a Look up the word 'miracle' in a dictionary.
    b Write a definition of a miracle.
3 Some Christians do not accept that there were only five loaves and two fishes. They believe that the miracle was that everyone sat down and shared their food. They believe that this is why there was enough food to feed five thousand people. If this was what happened, how would this event relate to the problem of hunger in the developing world? Explain your answer in detail.

Topic 1

What are work and leisure?

 What is ...?

Work is usually defined as the paid employment people undertake, or compulsory duties that have to be done.

 Activity

> Whatever you do, work at it with all your heart, as though you were working for the Lord and not for men.
>
> (Colossians 3:23)

1 List some of the reasons why people **work**.
2 List any work that you think that some Christians would believe is not 'working for the Lord'. For each example on your list, give a reason for your choice.

 What do you think?

Which do you think is the most important factor in choosing a job? Is it the pay, the working conditions or the job satisfaction? Can you think of other important factors? Explain your choice.

In the past, people believed that the harder you worked the better it was for you. They believed that the harder you worked then the greater would be God's reward. This was known as the **Protestant work ethic**.

The **Temperance Movement** developed at the end of the 19th century. People who joined this group signed a pledge not to drink any form of alcohol. The Temperance Movement began at a time of heavy drinking among the poorer workers. Those who had signed the pledge tended to gain promotion over those who continued to drink heavily. This reinforced the idea that God rewarded those who worked hard.

 What do you think?

Can you think of any other reasons besides a 'reward' from God that might have made those who did not drink alcohol more successful than those who spent each night in the public houses?

Some people believe that they must do a certain job, such as nursing or teaching. They may choose a job or career because they believe that they have been called to do it. Those who believe that they have a **vocation** choose the career not for the money or prospects, but because it is what they feel they have to do. Mother Teresa became a nun and worked with the dying in Calcutta because she felt called to serve God in this way.

In the past people only had time free from work to allow them to attend places of worship or to go on pilgrimage. These holy days were often linked to special festivals such as Christmas and Easter. Holy days gradually began to be linked to the idea of **leisure** time and the word changed to 'holidays'.

What is...?

A **vocation** is a 'calling' to a specific job or career. Christians believe this call has come from God, and that they must do a certain job or work. It may be a specialized calling, such as the priesthood, or simply to serve God in whatever they do.

Leisure is the time that one has free from compulsory duties. People are able to relax during leisure time.

How do you use your leisure time?

Activity

1 In pairs, discuss how you spend your leisure time.
2 Look up the following biblical references: Matthew 8:23–24; Luke 6:12; Luke 7:36; Luke 14:1; and John 2:1–3.
3 Using these Bible readings, write a paragraph describing the different ways in which Jesus used his leisure time.

Mother Teresa took a vow of poverty

Questions

1 Explain the differences between work and leisure.
2 **a** What is a vocation?
   b Give an example of a form of work that may be described as a vocation.
3 Explain the Protestant work ethic.
4 What is the origin of the word 'holiday'?
5 'A person with religious beliefs will work harder than someone with no religious beliefs.' Do you agree? Give reasons for your answer, showing that you have thought about more than one point of view.

Topic 2

Unemployment

Unemployment exists when someone who wants to work cannot find a suitable job for his or her skills.

Technology has reduced the number of employees that a firm needs

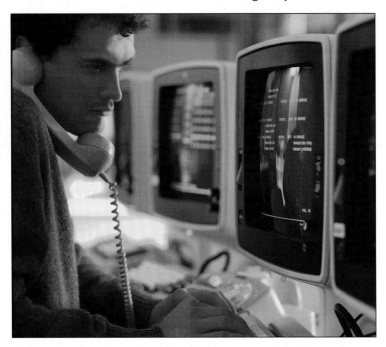

In the 1900s, over three million people were unemployed in Britain. There were many industrial towns where a high percentage of the population was out of work. Most Christians believe that helping those in need includes helping the unemployed.

The causes of unemployment

There are many causes of **unemployment**, some of which are listed below.

- The product made by a firm is no longer in demand and so the factory has to reduce its workforce.
- The introduction of technology means that a smaller workforce is needed. Robots and machines can now do many jobs. Computers are able to do the work of many people.
- The economy of the country or of the world enters a slump, and so there is less money to create new jobs.
- The population is rising and there are more people in the country looking for jobs.

Unemployment is not the same as leisure. Unemployment is something that people do not want. An unemployed person will not have any spare money to spend. Unemployment does not just affect the person who has lost his or her job, but it affects others as well. Unemployment affects families, communities and the whole country.

The effects of unemployment

There are many effects of unemployment. These include:

- There is less money in circulation if there is high unemployment. People buy less and so other shops and factories have to reduce their workforce.
- Long-term unemployment can lead to a loss of self-respect. Unemployed people feel of no use to themselves, their family or society. This can result in depression and even suicide.
- Unemployment may lead to friction between a couple. This could be the result of mounting debts, frustration at not getting a job or irritability because the unemployed person is always at home. The divorce rate increases with unemployment.
- An increase in crime is linked to unemployment. Vandalism is one way in which the unemployed take out their frustrations on a society that

Find out the current total number of people unemployed in Britain.

has failed to give them a job. The lack of a regular income leads people to steal to pay their debts.

- There is less income tax available to spend on health and education. This is because fewer people are paying tax and more people are receiving benefits.

Activity

'People should be made to do some form of community work to receive unemployment pay.' Imagine that the class is taking part in a phone-in programme on the local radio, with this statement as the topic. Each member of the class needs to take the part of someone who might ring in with a view on the topic, such as a Christian, an unemployed man, the mother of an unemployed teenager or a politician. A member of the class will need to be the radio presenter who responds to the listeners' comments, questions and the arguments that may develop between listeners.

Christians believe that they should help the unemployed. This may involve organizing luncheon clubs for the unemployed or holidays for their children. It could involve setting up training programmes so that the unemployed can learn a new skill. Many Christians believe the Church has a duty to put political pressure on the government to help with the creation of more jobs.

Unemployment leads to boredom

Questions

1 What is unemployment?
2 List **three** causes of unemployment.
3 List **three** effects of unemployment.
4 Why do you think that Christians believe they have a duty to help the unemployed? Support your answer with biblical teachings you have studied.
5 How could the following help to overcome the problems of unemployment:
   a an individual
   b the Church?
6 'Satan finds work for idle hands to do.'
   a What does this proverb mean?
   b To what extent and for what reasons do you think that unemployment may cause an increase in crime?
   c Do you think that having a religious faith will ease the problems caused by unemployment for an individual? Give reasons for your opinion.

Topic 3
The Christian response to work and leisure

What is...?

The **Sabbath** is a day set aside for rest and worship.

Sunday is a day of worship for Christians

It is important to Christians not only that they work in a manner which will please God, but also that they use their leisure time as a gift from God.

All Christians believe that Jesus saved the world from sin; there is one Church, one baptism and life after death. Christians agree that Jesus, as the Son of God, has complete authority. Christians have shared beliefs but choose to follow these beliefs in different ways. This is seen by the different ways in which Christians worship on the **Sabbath**.

The first Christians were Jews and continued to keep the Jewish Sabbath. There were very strict rules in Judaism about working on the Sabbath. The word 'sabbath' means rest, and no form of work was allowed. Jesus performed miracles on the Sabbath to heal the sick and was criticized by the Jewish leaders. Jesus replied that the Sabbath was made for man, not man for the Sabbath. He meant that God had created the Sabbath for the good of man. Jesus' teaching about the use of the Sabbath has influenced the way in which Christians behave on Sunday.

Gentiles (non-Jews) wanted to show that Christianity was a separate faith to Judaism. Sunday was chosen as their holy day because it was on the first Easter Sunday that Jesus rose from the dead. Some Christians still believe that Saturday is the Sabbath and a day of rest. This is because the commandment states that God made the world in six days and 'rested on the seventh', and the seventh day is Saturday. This group is called Seventh Day Adventists.

What do you think?

Some Christians believe that Sunday should be a day of complete rest. This would mean that Sunday trading would not be allowed.

Do you think that Sunday should be a day of rest or not? Give reasons for your answer, showing that you have thought about more than one point of view.

Christians use some of their leisure time for private worship. This includes prayer and reading the Bible. Christians believe that private prayer brings them closer to God and helps them to understand how God wants them to live their life.

Questions

   1 **a** Why was Sunday chosen as the Christian day of rest by the majority of Christians?
       b Suggest one way in which a Christian can show that Sunday is a holy day.
   2 Why do many Christians believe that worship together on Sundays is important?
   3 What is prayer?
   4 Why do many Christians believe that they should use some of their leisure time for private worship?

According to Christians, the teaching of Jesus makes it clear that if those in need are ignored then people are not behaving as God wishes. So Christians believe that some of their leisure time should be used to help others. This may involve taking part in fund-raising activities or helping people with disabilities. It could involve visiting the sick or the elderly, or helping people in other ways.

Activity

   1 Look back at the parable of the sheep and the goats on pages 60–61.
   2 List the groups of people who needed help which Jesus mentions in this parable.
   3 For each person on your list, suggest a way in which an individual could help him or her.

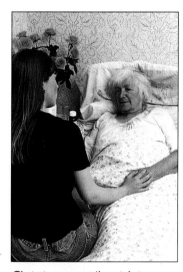

Christians must 'be rich in good works'

In his first letter to Timothy, St Paul explained that it is not wealth that matters with God, but how people use their time. God provides things for people to enjoy, but he also expects that people will use some time to benefit others.

God Commands People to do Good (I Timothy 6:17–19)

Command those who are rich in this present world not to be arrogant nor to put their hope in wealth, which is so uncertain, but to put their hope in God, who richly provides us with everything for our enjoyment. Command them to do good, to be rich in good deeds, and to be generous and willing to share. In this way they will lay up treasure for themselves as a firm foundation for the coming age, so that they may take hold of the life that is truly life.

Questions

   1 What does the parable of the sheep and the goats teach a Christian about the use of leisure?
   2 State and explain **three** ways in which Christians could use their leisure to help others.
   3 What did St Paul teach about 'good works' in his letter to Timothy?
   4 How do you think that modern Christians could apply this teaching to the use of their spare time? Support your answer with examples.

Topic 4

The use and abuse of leisure

The use of leisure

Christians are taught that leisure is to be used to serve God. Christians believe that some activities are acceptable to God, and that there are other activities of which God will disapprove.

What is ...?

A **talent** was a gold coin at the time of Jesus. The word has now come to mean a special skill or ability.

Activity

1 Look back at Topic 3: The Christian response to work and leisure.
2 List **three** ways which might be considered a good use of leisure time by a Christian.
3 List **three** ways which might be considered a waste of time or a misuse of leisure time by a Christian.

The Parable of the Talents (Matthew 25:14–30)

Again, it will be like a man going on a journey, who called his servants and entrusted his property to them. To one he gave five talents of money, to another two talents, and to another one talent, each according to his ability. Then he went on his journey. The man who had received the five talents went at once and put his money to work and gained five more. So also, the one with the two talents gained two more. But the man who had received the one talent went off, dug a hole in the ground and hid his master's money.

After a long time the master of those servants returned and settled accounts with them. The man who had received the five talents brought the other five. "Master," he said, "you entrusted me with five talents. See, I have gained five more."

His master replied, "Well done, good and faithful servant! You have been faithful with a few things; I will put you in charge of many things. Come and share your master's happiness!"

The man with the two talents also came. "Master," he said, "you entrusted me with two talents; see, I have gained two more."

His master replied, "Well done, good and faithful servant! You have been faithful with a few things; I will put you in charge of many things. Come and share your master's happiness!"

Then the man who had received the one talent came. "Master," he said, "I knew that you are a hard man, harvesting where you have not sown and gathering where you have not scattered. So I was afraid and went out and hid your talent in the ground. See, here is what belongs to you."

His master replied, "You wicked, lazy servant! So you knew that I harvest where I have not sown and gather where I have not scattered seed? Well then, you should have put my money on deposit with the bankers, so that when I returned I would have received it back with interest.

"Take the talent from him and give it to the one who has the ten talents. For everyone who has will be given more, and he will have an abundance. Whoever does not have, even what he has will be taken from him. And throw that worthless servant outside, into the darkness, where there will be weeping and gnashing of teeth."

Christians are encouraged to use some of their leisure time to find out what special skills God has given them. Jesus taught that God has given people special skills which they need to develop and use for the benefit of others.

 What do you think?

Using the word 'talent' to mean a special skill, what do you think that Jesus was trying to teach people about the use of their talents? Give reasons for your view.

 Activity

Outline the parable of the talents in your own words.

People's talents vary. Some people seem to be good at everything, whereas other people seem to have only one skill. One interpretation of the parable is that Jesus is teaching that however many gifts (talents) people have, these must be used and developed.

People could practise and improve these skills in leisure time as well as at work. People might use leisure time to discover any new skills they may possess, such as playing a sport, learning to paint or joining a drama group.

 Activity

In class, brainstorm all the leisure activities of the students. As each activity is written down, discuss how people became involved in the activity. Try to think of any benefits or harm that could result from these activities.

Christians believe that having found a special skill or talent then it must be used for the benefit of others. This may take a variety of forms. A Christian who is a good runner may take part in a sponsored run to raise money for charity. A musical talent may lead another Christian to give concerts to entertain people in hospital or old people's homes. Many playgroups to occupy children during the school holidays are organized by students in their summer break.

Members of the Salvation Army make it a rule never to drink alcohol

The abuse of leisure

Chrisians differ in their views about leisure activities. For example, members of the Salvation Army would argue that many of the evils in society are linked to alcohol, and therefore its use must not be encouraged. Other Christians argue that alcohol, if taken in moderation, is acceptable. They believe that as Jesus and St Paul drank wine then they can do so too.

What do you think?

Do you agree with those Christians who believe that alcohol is a cause of evil and should be avoided? Give reasons for your opinion.

Some Christians are against any forms of gambling and oppose the National Lottery. They believe that, as with alcohol, gambling can lead to addiction and misery. They believe gambling is a leisure time activity that should be avoided.

There are other activities that all Christians believe is a misuse of leisure. In the following extract from a letter to the Ephesians, St Paul is telling Christians how to behave and which activities to avoid. He is warning Christians to avoid people who spend much of their time in pointless activities.

Living as Children of Light (Ephesians 5:3–18)

But among you there must not be even a hint of sexual immorality, or of any kind of impurity, or of greed, because these are improper for God's holy people. Nor should there be obscenity, foolish talk or coarse joking, which are out of place, but rather thanksgiving. For of this you can be sure: No immoral, impure or greedy person – such a man is an idolater – has any inheritance in the kingdom of Christ and of God. Let no one deceive you with empty words, for because of such things God's wrath comes on those who are disobedient. Therefore do not be partners with them.

For you were once darkness, but now you are light in the Lord. Live as children of light (for the fruit of the light consists in all goodness, righteousness and truth) and find out what pleases the Lord. Have nothing to do with the fruitless deeds of darkness, but rather expose them. For it is shameful even to mention what the disobedient do in secret. But everything exposed by the light becomes visible, for it is light that makes everything visible. This is why it is said:

"Wake up, O sleeper,
rise from the dead,
and Christ will shine on you."

Be very careful, then, how you live – not as unwise but as wise, making the most of every opportunity, because the days are evil. Therefore do not be foolish, but understand what the Lord's will is. Do not get drunk on wine, which leads to debauchery. Instead, be filled with the Spirit.

What do you think?

1 What sort of activities in the modern world do you think St Paul would describe as 'obscenity, foolish talk or coarse joking'?
2 Why do you think St Paul would believe that these activities are to be avoided? Give reasons for your opinion.

Boredom might be one cause of the foolish activities St Paul describes. Is vandalism the result of boredom?

Christians believe that illegal drug taking is a misuse of leisure. They believe God would not approve of it, because it damages the body and can become addictive. Drugs can lead people to steal to support their addiction.

Christians may oppose drugs, alcohol and gambling, but some use their leisure time to help those who have become addicted to these activities. This is another example of Christians hating the sin but showing love for the sinner.

Activity

David Wilkerson is an example of a Christian whose vocation led him to work with the violent teenage gangs of New York. He succeeded in saving many of them from a life of drug addiction and crime. His work was made into a film called *The Cross and the Switchblade*.

1 Find out about the work of an individual Christian or Christian organization which seeks to overcome the problems of drugs, alcohol, gambling or vandalism.
2 Write up your findings to present a five-minute talk to your class about the individual or organization. It is important to show in your talk how Christian beliefs have influenced the work of the individual or organization.

Questions

1 Explain why Christians believe that drinking alcohol to access is wrong.
2 Why might some people believe that 'hanging around' street corners is a misuse of leisure? Give reasons and examples to support your answer.
3 Why do some people believe that they should help those addicted to drugs, alcohol or gambling? Give as many reasons as possible.

Do you understand...
the Christian response to work and leisure?

Task 1

> Do not take advantage of a hired man who is poor and needy, whether he is a brother Israelite or an alien living in one of your towns. Pay him his wages each day before sunset, because he is poor and is counting on it. Otherwise he may cry to the Lord against you, and you will be guilty of sin.
>
> **(Deuteronomy 24:14–15)**

1 What is this passage recommending to employers about the payment of wages?
2 How might this passage apply to the import of goods from the developing world?

Task 2

St Paul said, 'If a man will not work, he shall not eat'
(2 Thessalonians 3:10).

1 Do you think that St Paul meant any unemployed person should not be fed, or only those who refuse to get a job? Give reasons for your view.
2 Explain the problems unemployment causes for both the unemployed person and society as a whole.
3 How could Christians help the unemployed? Give specific examples.
4 Why do Christians believe that they should help the unemployed? Support your answer with biblical teaching.

Task 3

1 The fourth commandment states: 'Remember the Sabbath day by keeping it holy. Six days you shall labour and do all your work, but the seventh day is a Sabbath to the Lord your God. On it you shall not do any work' (Exodus 20:8–10).
   a Explain why God expects people to keep the Sabbath holy.
   b Why have most Christians chosen Sunday as their holy day?
2 List some of the ways in which an individual Christian might spend Sundays.
3 'Family shopping is one way in which people can rest and relax together on Sundays. Jesus would have approved.' Do you agree? Give reasons for your answer, showing that you have thought about more than one point of view.

Task 4

1 Why might the effects of old age lead to boredom for some elderly people? Give specific examples to support your answer.
2 In what ways could older people help younger people?
3 How could younger people use their talents to help older people?
4 What could local churches do to help the elderly? Give examples in your answer.

How can younger people help older people?

Task 5

Look back at St Paul's teaching on the payment of taxes in Romans 13:1–7 (see page 33).
1 Why does St Paul believe that Christians should pay their taxes?
2 What are taxes used for in Britain today?
3 'A little tax dodging is all right if you do not get caught.' Do you agree with this statement? Give reasons for your opinion, showing that you have thought about more than one point of view.

Task 6

The report 'Young People in 1997' has discovered that more teenagers are smoking and drinking alcohol than in previous surveys. The report gave no evidence to suggest an increase in the number of teenagers taking illegal drugs.

1 The number of girls who smoke is now greater than the number of boys. Why do you think more girls are smoking than boys?
2 Why do you think that there is an increase in underage drinking?
3 Why do you think that the number of teenagers taking illegal drugs has not increased?
4 Why do some Christians believe that the use of drugs, alcohol and tobacco by teenagers is wrong?
5 How could teenage involvement with drugs be reduced?
6 Why do some Christians believe that they should try to help young people with problems?

Almost a third of girls aged 14 to 15 said they smoked

Task 7

1 In what ways might an addiction to gambling affect:
   a family life;
   b job prospects;
   c the crime rate?
2 'Lottery tickets and scratch cards are just harmless fun. They entertain the public.' Do you agree? Give reasons for your answer, showing that you have thought about more than one point of view.

® Revision

Check list

Before you begin your revision, you need to check the following points with your teacher.

- You need to know which examination board's syllabus you have studied.
- You need to know how the syllabus will expect you to use the information and knowledge you have studied in this book.
- You need to know which biblical passages the examination board expects you to have studied in detail.
- You need to know the format of the examination paper. Will you have to answer all questions or will there be a choice? Will there be different types of questions, ranging from short answers to essays?
- You need to know the date, time and length of the examination paper.

Careful revision brings success

Preparation

Once you have all this information from your teacher, you need to organize your notes. Make sure that you have covered all the topics in the syllabus. If you have any information missing, make sure that you copy up the work.

Revision timetable

Organize your revision time carefully. It is never too early to start revision. Work out how many weeks are left before your 'mock' examination or the GCSE examinations start. Make a plan of all the topics you need to revise and all the leisure activities you wish to continue during the revision period. Fill in study periods and leisure periods. At the beginning of each week decide which topics you are going to study during that week.

Allow some flexibility in your timetable, as you do not know what unexpected events may happen. **Do not leave revision to the last minute.**

Make the best use of revision time

- You need a suitable environment in which to revise. Some people need to revise in total silence, whereas other people like music in the background. Use whichever method helps your revision.
- You need to get down to work according to the timetable **you** have drawn up. Revise the topic you have written down, and do not waste time deciding what you are going to do.
- Sitting staring at a page or set of notes is not the best use of revision time.

Revision techniques

Successful revision involves active learning. There are a variety of revision techniques which can help you to understand and memorize information. You need to find which technique is best for you.

Note-taking
- Summaries of your work can help you remember the information. As you study each section of your notes, write down the important points.
- Learn these points and then cover up the notes and rewrite them from memory.
- Check off your list from memory against your original list, and note any points you got wrong or forgot to include.

Practise past questions
- Use past questions you have worked through in class, or questions from past examination papers, to help you understand the work.
- Answer the questions, in note form, using your notes.
- Cover up your answer and work through the question again without notes.
- Check off your answer from memory against your original list, and note any points you got wrong or forgot to include.

Use the 'Do you understand' sections of this book
Work through each set of tasks in each of the sections in this book to help you to develop your skills and understanding.

Ask relatives and friends to test you
Give them your notes and ask them to test you on the information. Make sure that they tell you the right answer, if you get questions wrong.

Final preparation

- Make sure that you have a good night's sleep before the examination.
- Take several pens and pencils into the examination room.
- Read the examination questions carefully and do not rush your answers.
- If you have time at the end of the examination then check through your answers.